Excel

YEARS 9 to 10

Writing and Spelling Workbook

ESSENTIAL skills

Get the Results You Want!

Bianca Hewes

Reprinted 2019, 2023

ISBN 978 1 74125 415 0

Pascal Press
PO Box 250
Glebe NSW 2037
(02) 9198 1748
www.pascalpress.com.au

Publisher: Vivienne Joannou
Series developer and consultant: Kristine Brown
Project editors: Mark Dixon and Rosemary Peers
Edited by Rosemary Peers
Reviewed by Cassandra Freeman
Typeset by Grizzly Graphics (Leanne Richters)
Cover and page design by DiZign Pty Ltd
Printed by Vivar Printing/Green Giant Press

Contents

Imaginative texts

To the student

This book is designed to help you master the main language features and structures of some very common types of texts that you will encounter in school and in your life. Each chapter is designed to guide you through the process of planning, drafting and then writing a specific type of text. Take your time when completing the activities in each chapter as these will help you compose a stronger piece of writing at the end.

Each text will be persuasive, informative or imaginative. The marking criteria section (pages vi–viii) outlines the features of advanced, intermediate and basic levels of writing. It's a good idea to read these criteria carefully so that you know what features are expected in a high-quality response.

Each chapter is divided into six sections. The exercises and examples in each chapter relate directly to the type of text that you are being asked to write.

- ***Understanding the question****—each chapter opens with a question asking you to write a specific type of text. This section gets you thinking about the type of question you have been asked. You will complete a couple of small activities about the chapter question.*
- ***Planning and organisation****—this section will help you plan the content for your piece of writing.*
- ***Structure****—this section will focus on the specific structure required for the type of text you have been asked to write.*
- ***Language feature****—this section focuses on the main language feature you will need to know and master for the type of text you have been asked to write.*
- ***Spotlight on spelling****—this section will give you the opportunity to identify spelling rules to help develop your spelling skills.*
- ***You be the teacher****—in this section you will look at a paragraph of a student's writing and make corrections based on the structure and spelling rules you have mastered in earlier sections of this chapter.*
- ***Now you write****—it is time for you to put into practice everything you have just learned about this specific text type. You will now write your answer to the chapter question using the required type of text.*
- ***Looking at other students' writing****—you are given an example of a student's writing to look at closely. This is an advanced piece of writing which is annotated to help you see the strengths of the student's writing and help guide you with your own writing.*

By the end of each chapter, you will have composed a complete and extended piece of writing. Writing should be an enjoyable and creative process, so I hope you enjoy this book!

Bianca Hewes

Marking criteria

Persuasive texts

Criteria	Advanced	Intermediate	Basic
Content: appropriateness to audience	• The text skilfully engages and persuades the audience. • The text uses an excellent selection and elaboration of ideas relevant to the persuasive text topic. • A wide variety of persuasive devices (such as rhetorical questions, repetition, strong verbs and adverbs) have been used to enhance the writer's position and persuade the audience to accept this position.	• The text engages and persuades the audience reasonably well. • There is sound selection and some elaboration of ideas relevant to the persuasive text topic. • Attempts have been made to use persuasive devices (such as rhetorical questions, repetition, high modal adverbs) to enhance the writer's position and persuade the audience to accept this position.	• The text fails to engage and persuade the audience. • The writing shows a weak selection and minimal elaboration of ideas relevant to the persuasive text topic. • Few persuasive devices have been used.
Mechanics: punctuation, spelling, sentence structure, vocabulary	• A wide range of precise and appropriate language choices have been made—specifically vocabulary relevant to the text topic. • All sentences are grammatically correct, structurally sound and meaningful. • All punctuation is correct. • All words are spelt correctly, including more complex and technical spelling words.	• Language choices are appropriate to the text topic but lack detail. • Most sentences are grammatically correct, structurally sound and meaningful. • Most punctuation is correct but there are some errors. • Most words are spelt correctly but there are some errors.	• Language choices may be inappropriate and not relevant to the text topic. • Sentences are unclear and contain obvious grammatical errors. • There are frequent punctuation errors. • There are frequent spelling errors and vocabulary is basic.
Form: text structure, paragraphing, cohesion	• The text has a highly effective structure appropriate to a persuasive text including an introduction, body and conclusion. • Connectives (e.g. *also*, *similarly*, *furthermore*) are used effectively for smooth and coherent transition between the main points in the text. • Highly effective division of the persuasive text into paragraphs is used to help the audience to follow the line of argument.	• Appropriate structure for a persuasive text is used, including introduction, body and conclusion, but may be disorganised or too short. • Attempts have been made to use connectives (e.g. *also*, *similarly*, *furthermore*) for smooth and coherent transition between the main points in the text. • The text is divided into paragraphs that help the audience to follow the line of argument.	• The speech is missing some or all of the required structural components. • Connectives (e.g. *also*, *similarly*, *furthermore*) are not used or are used inappropriately. • The text is not divided into paragraphs or the paragraphs are infrequent.

Informative texts

Criteria	Advanced	Intermediate	Basic
Content: appropriateness to audience	• The text skilfully engages and informs the audience. • The text uses an excellent selection and elaboration of ideas relevant to the informative text. • A wide variety of informative devices (such as objective language, headings, topic sentences, definitions, supporting evidence and factual tone) have been used to explain the topic of the informative text.	• The text engages and informs the audience reasonably well. • There is sound selection and some elaboration of ideas relevant to the persuasive speech topic. • Attempts have been made to use informative devices (such as objective language, headings, topic sentences, definitions, supporting evidence and factual tone) to explain the topic of the informative text.	• The text fails to engage and inform the audience. • The writing shows a weak selection and minimal elaboration of ideas relevant to the informative text. • Few informative devices have been used.
Mechanics: punctuation, spelling, sentence structure, vocabulary	• A wide range of precise and appropriate language choices have been made—specifically vocabulary relevant to the topic. • All sentences are grammatically correct, structurally sound and meaningful. • All punctuation is correct. • All words are spelt correctly, including more complex and technical spelling words.	• Language choices are appropriate to the topic but lack detail. • Most sentences are grammatically correct, structurally sound and meaningful. • Most punctuation is correct but there are some errors. • Most words are spelt correctly but there are some errors.	• Language choices may be inappropriate and not relevant to the topic. • Sentences are unclear and contain obvious grammatical errors. • There are frequent punctuation errors. • There are frequent spelling errors and the vocabulary used is basic.
Form: text structure, paragraphing, cohesion	• The text has a highly effective structure appropriate to the informative type of text. • Connectives and conjunctions (e.g. *also*, *similarly*, *furthermore*) are used effectively for smooth and coherent transition between the main parts of the informative text. • Highly effective division of the informative text into paragraphs is used to help the audience to follow the key pieces of information.	• Appropriate structure for an informative type of text is used but may be disorganised or too short. • Attempts have been made to use connectives and conjunctions (e.g. *also*, *similarly*, *furthermore*) for smooth and coherent transition between the main points in the speech. • The text is divided into paragraphs that help the audience to follow the key pieces of information.	• The text is missing some or all of the required structural components. • Connectives and conjunctions (e.g. *also*, *similarly*, *furthermore*) are not used or are used inappropriately. • The text is not divided into paragraphs or the paragraphs are infrequent.

Imaginative texts

Criteria	Advanced	Intermediate	Basic
Content: audience, narrative devices, ideas	• The text skilfully engages the audience in experiences, events or characters. • There is excellent development of real or imagined experiences or events using relevant descriptive details. • A wide variety of narrative devices (such as dialogue, description, figurative language and mood) have been used to develop experiences, events and/or characters.	• The text engages the audience reasonably well in experiences, events or characters. • There is sound development of real or imagined experiences or events using relevant descriptive details. • Attempts have been made to use narrative devices (such as dialogue, description, figurative language and mood) to develop experiences, events and/or characters.	• The text fails to engage the audience. • There is weak development of real or imagined experiences or events using relevant descriptive details. • Few narrative devices have been used.
Mechanics: punctuation, spelling, sentence structure, vocabulary	• A wide range of precise and appropriate language choices have been made—specifically descriptive details and sensory language relevant to the topic. • All sentences are grammatically correct, structurally sound and meaningful. • All punctuation is correct. • All words are spelt correctly, including more complex and challenging spelling words.	• Language choices are appropriate to the topic but lack detail. • Most sentences are grammatically correct, structurally sound and meaningful. • Most punctuation is correct but there are some errors. • Most words are spelt correctly but there are some errors.	• Language choices may be inappropriate and not relevant to the topic. • Sentences are unclear and contain obvious grammatical errors. • There are frequent punctuation errors. • There are frequent spelling errors and vocabulary is basic.
Form: text structure, paragraphing, cohesion	• This text has a highly effective structure appropriate to the narrative type of text. • A variety of transition words, phrases and/or clauses convey sequence and signal shifts from one time frame or setting to another. • Highly effective division of the text into paragraphs helps the audience to follow the key elements of the narrative.	• Appropriate structure for a narrative type of text is used but may be disorganised or too short. • A variety of transition words, phrases and/or clauses are used to convey sequence and signal shifts from one time frame or setting to another. • The text is segmented into paragraphs that help the audience follow the key elements of the narrative.	• The text is missing some or all of the required structural components. • The text uses few, if any, transition words, phrases and/or clauses to convey sequence and signal shifts from one time frame or setting to another. • The text is not divided into paragraphs or the paragraphs are infrequent.

UNIT ONE

Persuasive texts

Argument essays

Understanding the question

Write an argument addressing the question below:
Should parents let teenagers make their own decisions?

Type of question

This question is asking you to write a particular type of response—an **argument essay**.

How do you know an argument essay is wanted and not an informative essay? The word *should* is the clue. It shows you are required to **adopt a position** on the topic—a point of view. Here you are being asked to adopt a position arguing **for** or **against** parents letting teenagers make their own decisions.

Features of an argument essay

- Aims to influence or convince the audience to agree with the speaker
- Argues for or against a particular issue
- Provides arguments to support a particular point of view
- Supports ideas with evidence
- Has a broad structure: introduction, body and conclusion
- Uses persuasive language

1 What are some **decisions** that might be best made by parents for teenagers? For example: which high school to attend.

a ______________________________

b ______________________________

c ______________________________

2 List four types of **decisions** that teenagers might want to make independently of their parents.

a ______________________________

b ______________________________

c ______________________________

d ______________________________

TIP A convincing argument essay has a thoughtful argument that is supported by strong evidence. Spend time carefully planning your essay, as this will help you clarify your ideas and ensure you use convincing evidence.

Planning and organisation

You must **plan** before every piece of writing you do.

Planning is important because it helps you:

* **develop and organise your ideas** in response to the question
* ensure you are **keeping to the task** and type of text.

Activity 1

Complete the following table to identify reasons **for** and **against** teenagers being allowed to make their own decisions. Make sure you focus on **reasons** for each position. Don't simply list types of decisions that parents or teenagers might want or need to make.

Question: Should parents let teenagers make their own decisions?	
For	**Against**

Activity 2

Looking at the information above, think now about which side you agree with most strongly. In other words, decide your **position** on the topic. Your position will have you stating that you either are **for** or **against** teenagers making their own decisions. However, it is important to keep in mind that with a **persuasive essay** your position may have some conditions, such as *Parents should make all of the decisions. However, if parents are not around, teenagers may be forced to make decisions for themselves.*

Use the mind-map below to expand your argument. You will need to include your position and your reasons for adopting this position, as well as evidence to support your position.

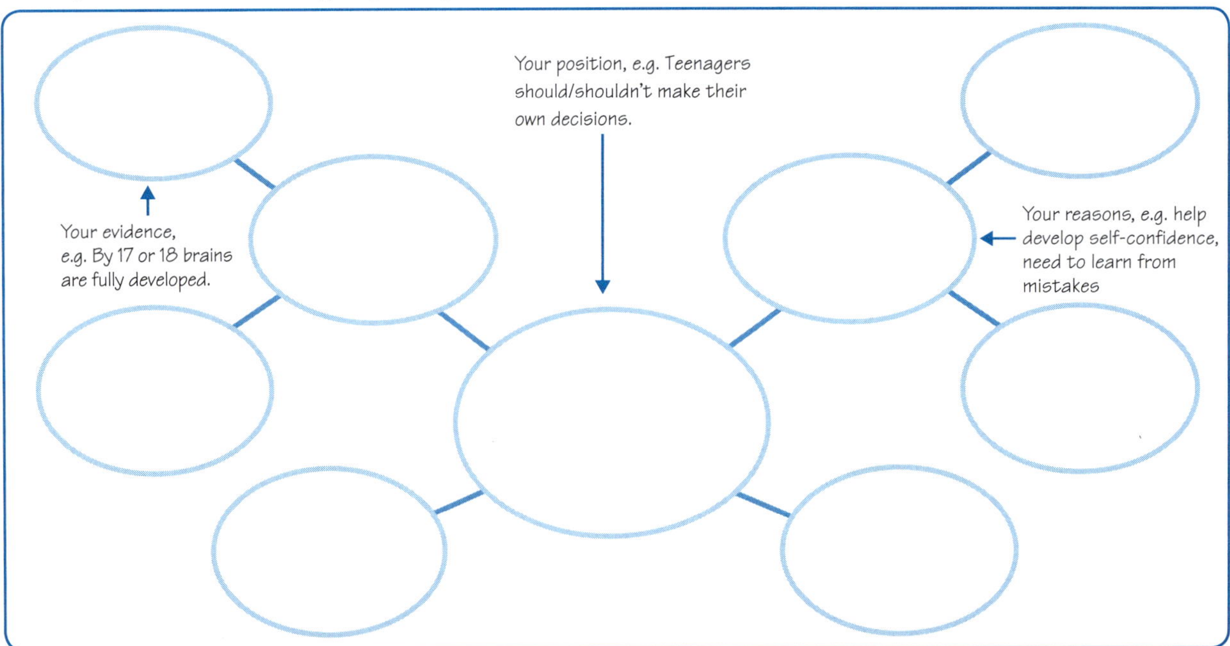

Structure

The **structure** of an **argument essay** is very similar to the structure of other more formal essays. An argument essay has three main parts: **introductory** paragraph, **body** paragraphs and **concluding** paragraph. The difference between an argument essay and an informative essay is the purpose; this affects the type of language used. Argument essays aim to persuade readers to agree with the arguments and therefore **use language to persuade**.

Introductory paragraph

The purpose of an introduction is to clearly **outline** your topic and to state your **position** on this topic. An effective introduction for an argument essay should:

* **provide a brief explanation** of the topic, any relevant background information and define key terms where necessary
* **indicate your position** on the topic by outlining your thesis (one or two sentences that sum up what your essay will be about in relation to the essay topic)
* **include your three main arguments** to support this thesis.

Activity 1

a Read the sample **introduction** below and then complete the following tasks.

* Identify any relevant **background information** on the topic.
* Put an asterisk near the **definition of key terms**.
* Underline the writer's **thesis**.
* Number the three main **arguments** outlined to support the writer's thesis.

The world is rapidly changing and evolving. The number one factor in this change is technology. The number of technological innovations in the last 100 years is astounding. One of the consequences of living in a technology-saturated world is the possibility of becoming overly dependent on it, meaning people feel the need to rely on it for support, or even survival. There is evidence to suggest that people today are becoming increasingly dependent on technology, with potentially serious consequences. People have become overly reliant on digital entertainment, mobile phones and domestic appliances.

b What do you think is the **essay question** that this introduction is responding to? Give reasons for your answer.

Activity 2

It is now time for you to draft the **introduction** to your argument essay on the following topic: *Should parents let teenagers make their own decisions?* Remember to revise the structure of an introduction before you begin!

Body paragraphs

The **body** of an **argument essay** contains all of the important information that will support your argument. Each paragraph should focus on one of your main points, supported by evidence and/or explanation. You might choose to include one paragraph that refutes a possible argument from someone taking the opposing position.

The following is a suggested structure for each **body paragraph**. You can use the **SEW** acronym to help you remember the important parts.

Statement: Begin with a strong and clear statement on one of the three reasons for your position (already identified during the planning stage). Provide further detail about this statement in your second sentence.

Evidence: In one or two sentences, provide evidence or an example to support this statement. The evidence may take the form of a statistic, a quote from an article or the description of a personal experience.

Why: Your concluding sentence should explain why this reason and evidence support the position you have adopted on the topic.

Activity 3

In the following example of a good body paragraph:

a highlight the **Statement**

b underline the **Evidence**

c put a circle around the **Why**.

Mobile phones are one piece of technology that people are definitely addicted to. The number of mobile phones used around the world continues to rise. According to FoneBank Australia, over 88% of Australians own a mobile phone. Mobile phones are now so technologically advanced that they allow people to access the internet, listen to music, use GPS, take video and pictures, play video games and even monitor their own heart rate. Many people spend hours on their phones each day—using them when they are at dinner, at the movies, driving and even on the toilet! Mobile phones are definitely one form of technology that people are far too dependent on.

Activity 4

Go back to the notes you made during the planning stage. Use these to draft one **body paragraph** for your argument essay. Remember to use the SEW structure!

Concluding paragraph

The **concluding paragraph** of an argument essay is important because it provides you with an opportunity to restate and reinforce your position on the topic. An effective conclusion will:

- **restate** your position on the topic—**for** or **against** the issue (this is your thesis)
- **summarise** your three main **arguments** for holding this position
- **refer** briefly to the **reservations** you have about your position, such as when and why your position may not be entirely valid
- **include** a final sentence that quotes someone well known saying something relevant to your topic.

Activity 5

Draft the **concluding paragraph** for your argument essay, checking that you have included all four of the above elements.

Language feature

Third person

Most essays that you will write will be in the **third person**. The third person is the **use of pronouns such as *he*, *she*, *it*** and ***they*** and the avoidance of first-person pronouns, such as *I*, *we* and *us*, or the second-person pronoun *you*. Argument essays, because they are persuasive in nature, are typically written in the third person as this gives them a more **objective tone**, meaning that you have considered the facts and are not presenting a personal or biased account. When writing in the third person, nouns and common nouns are often used instead of pronouns.

For example:

First person: I think parents should let children make their own decisions.

Third person: Parents should give children the freedom to make their own decisions.

The third-person pronouns and possessive pronouns you might need when writing essays are: *he, she, it, they, them, him, his, her, its, their, hers* and *theirs.*

The first- and second-person pronouns and possessive pronouns you should **avoid** are: *I, me, my, you, your, we, us, our, mine, yours* and *ours.*

Activity 1

Change the following sentences from the first person to the **third person**. You may be able to do this by just taking out some words.

a My belief is that people today are too obsessed with technology.

b In no way do I feel that the death penalty is ever acceptable.

c My family, like many other families, uses a lot of technology.

Activity 2

Change the underlined words into the **third person** in these sentences and take out inappropriate personal references. This requires you to change some of the pronouns and possessive pronouns, and replace some with nouns. The first one has been done for you.

a We have enjoyed watching the evolution of Beyonce's music and fashion style.

Many people have enjoyed watching the evolution of Beyonce's music and fashion style.

b My family speaks highly of the impact of technology on learning.

c Take this opportunity and make your voice heard.

d The closing of the bridge will affect our ability to arrive at work on time.

e Nothing has been quite as devastating as the loss of my pet dog, Bart.

f It is my firm belief that people must respect one another, regardless of gender or race.

Activity 3

Read the passage below and underline the words that place it in the first person. Then use the given space to rewrite the passage in the **third person**. This requires you to change some of the pronouns and possessive pronouns, and replace some with nouns.

American filmmaker Spike Jonze is, I believe, the most creative and innovative director of the 21st century. I love how his films focus on subcultures and the human psyche. They all inspire me to think in new ways about society and myself. Jonze's films are, for me, a portal into secret worlds.

Prefixes

Prefixes are attached to the beginning of a root word. They are frequently used to change the meaning of a root word to its opposite. Prefixes that do this are called **negative prefixes**.

For example: **dis**engage, **un**happy, **ir**responsible

Common negative prefixes are *un, in, dis, im, ir, de* and *il*. Note that *im* always goes before words starting with *b, m* or *p* and that *ir* only goes before words beginning with *r*.

Three points will help your **spelling** of words which begin with a **prefix**.

- The spelling of the **root** word never changes.
- The spelling of the **prefix** never changes and there is no doubling or adding of letters before they join to the root word.

  For example:

  The word *disconnect* has one *s*, not two.

  dis + connect → **dis**connect

- Some words end up with **double letters** but that is because the root word begins with the letter which ends the prefix.

  For example:

  ir + regular → **ir**regular

  il + legal → **il**legal

Activity 1

Add a **negative prefix** to each of the following words to create a word with the opposite meaning:

a joint ____________________

b empower ____________________

c construct ____________________

d value ____________________

e logical ____________________

f appropriate ____________________

g capable ____________________

h responsible ____________________

Activity 2

Choose the correct **prefix** from the box for each root word and then write the new word on the line beside it.

a regular	______________________	*im*
b possible	______________________	*dis*
c mobile	______________________	*un*
d embody	______________________	*un*
e happy	______________________	*im*
f natural	______________________	*ir*

Activity 3

Find the spelling errors in the sentences below. Write the correct spelling of each word on the line.

a The rate at which young people are becoming addicted to energy drinks is imppossible to calculate. ______________

b Decconstruction of Shakespeare's works is often seen as boring by students. ______________

c Parents need to emppower their children to make wise decisions independently. ______________

d It is a shame that the government is deevaluing art spaces in the local community. ______________

e Many believe it is innappropriate for teenagers to choose their subjects in senior school. ______________

f Labor has been un-happy with the popularity of their latest leader. ______________

You be the teacher

Below is a **body paragraph** for an argument essay written by a Year 9 student. There are some errors in the structure of the paragraph and the spelling of some words with prefixes. Can you correct the mistakes? Rewrite the paragraph with the **correct SEW structure** and with the **correct spelling of all words**.

Secrets should be respected, as long as they do not relate to ilegal or iresponsible activities. Decisions are difficult to make yet sometimes this difficulty must be endured by teenagers alone. Consequently, parents are unable to make decisions relating to secrets, therefore teenagers must be allowed to make decisions for themselves. It is immpossible for parents to know everything about teenagers' lives, because teenagers often have secrets that are too embarrassing or personal to share with their parents.

____

____

____

____

____

____

Now you write

It is now time for you to complete your own **argument essay** on the teenager decisions essay question.

1 Before you write, take some time to look at the student writing sample on the following page as a guide to writing standards.

2 Once you have read the student writing sample, take some time to think about what you believe are the most important features of an argument essay that you need to master. Use the lines below to jot down your answer to this question:
What do you find most difficult when writing this kind of text?

3 Now look at the persuasive text marking criteria on page vi to double-check that you understand the requirements for a really good piece of persuasive writing.

Remember that you have already done your planning and drafted your introduction, one body paragraph and conclusion. Use the lines below and your own paper. Good luck!

Looking at other students' writing

Write an argument essay addressing the question below:
Are we too dependent on technology?

ADVANCED SAMPLE

ARE WE TOO DEPENDENT ON TECHNOLOGY?

The world is rapidly changing and evolving. The number one factor in this change is technology. The number of technological innovations in the last 100 years is astounding. One of the consequences of living in a technology-saturated world is the possibility of becoming overly dependent on it, meaning people feel the need to rely on it for support or even survival. There is evidence to suggest that people today are becoming increasingly dependent on technology, with potentially serious consequences. They have become overly reliant on digital entertainment, mobile phones and domestic appliances.

Digital entertainment has become so advanced that many people feel they cannot live without it. Digital entertainment takes many forms, including video games, ebooks, on-demand television and social media. These people don't even need to wait a week for the next episode of their favourite television series—they can use a popular service like iTunes or Netflix to download a whole season. Watching an entire season in one sitting is so common these days that it even has a name: binge viewing. If people can't even wait a week to see a show, it is clear that they are far too dependent on technology.

Mobile phones are one piece of technology that people are definitely addicted to. The number of mobile phones used around the world continues to rise. According to FoneBank Australia, over 88% of Australians own a mobile phone. Mobile phones are now so advanced that they allow people to access the internet, listen to music, use GPS, take video and pictures, play video games and even monitor their own heart rate. Many people spend hours on their phones each day—using them when they are at dinner, at the movies, driving and even on the toilet! Mobile phones are definitely one form of technology that people are far too dependent on.

Finally, every household has many different appliances to make life easier for people. Household appliances that people take for granted include televisions, irons, kettles, microwaves and washing machines. These days many people no longer have the skills to wash clothes by hand. Similarly, it would be impossible for most people to live without a refrigerator. This shows that people are highly dependent on technological appliances in their homes.

As a result of our rapidly advancing technology-rich world, people have become far too dependent on technology. Some of the most common types of technology that people have become dependent on are digital entertainment, mobile phones and domestic appliances. Technology has become so common that people use it without thinking. However, there are dangers with this, as noted by author Nassim Taleb: 'The difference between technology and slavery is that slaves are fully aware that they are not free.'

Introduction
The introduction immediately alerts the audience to the topic of the essay: technology dependence. The first few short sentences engage the audience. The thesis and thesis points are clear.

Persuasive techniques
The student uses many modal words to show certainty and enforce point of view. Emotive words reinforce the student's position. Statistics support the argument.

Text structure
The student uses the correct structure of an argument essay: introduction, supporting paragraphs and conclusion.

Paragraphing
Each paragraph features one basic reason to support the author's point of view and evidence to support this reason. The student effectively uses the SEW paragraph structure. The conclusion is strong and includes all required elements.

Vocabulary
Language choices are appropriate to the student's purpose—to convince the reader that people are too dependent on technology. Complex and precise words are used to talk about the topic.

Sentence structure
All sentences are grammatically correct, well structured and meaningful, and use a variety of sentence patterns.

Ideas
Ideas are well selected and relevant with a lot of detail to support the student's position that we are too dependent on technology.

Cohesion
Connecting words show clear connections between ideas (e.g. *similarly*).

Punctuation
Correct punctuation is used throughout the argument.

Spelling
All words are spelt correctly.

UNIT TWO

Persuasive texts

Opinion pieces

Understanding the question

Write an opinion piece on climate change.

Type of question

This question is asking you to write a particular type of persuasive text—an **opinion piece**. Examples of opinion pieces are newspaper editorials, letters to the editor and blog posts. Sometimes you may hear this type of writing referred to as a **polemic**. Writing an opinion piece requires you to **adopt a position** on the topic—a point of view. Here, you are being asked to adopt a position on climate change.

Features of an opinion piece

- Aims to provoke an emotional or intellectual response from the reader about a controversial or current topic
- Often aims to influence the way people think or behave
- Should be highly engaging
- Can present a biased or personal view of an issue
- Paragraphs are usually loosely structured
- Uses highly persuasive language
- Uses a wide range of language features, including rhetorical questions, descriptive language and high modality
- Uses a variety of sentence types

1 Define the word *opinion*.

2 What do you personally understand *climate change* to be?

3 List five current controversial issues people might write **opinion pieces** about.

Planning and organisation

Activity 1

Research climate change on the internet. Use your findings to complete the table below.

Definition of climate change	
Reasons why people believe in climate change	
Reasons why people don't believe in climate change	

Activity 2

This writing task is quite open. You have been asked to write an opinion piece on climate change, which allows you to focus on any aspect of the climate change debate that you (or someone else) might feel passionate about. Below is a list of ideas about climate change that you may wish to focus on. Rank them from 1 to 5, with 1 being the idea you're most interested in.

- Food prices are expected to rise because of changing temperatures and the impact this has on the cost of growing food.
- It can make it even harder for people already living below the poverty line to grow edible crops.
- Over most of Earth's history, natural processes have been responsible for periods of climate change.
- Human activity may be responsible for the speeding up of climate change, particularly the use of non-renewable resources like coal and natural gas.
- The worst impacts of climate change, such as radical weather patterns and rising sea levels, can only be prevented by human actions.

A highly effective opinion piece is designed to be current and provocative, and will therefore draw on evidence from current events, research and your own personal experiences.

Activity 3

Now that you have a good understanding of the issue, it's time to decide on your **opinion** of climate change. Choose three **reasons** from your list above to support your opinion and write them in the table below. Elaborate on each reason with **evidence** from your research or from your own life experiences.

Reason one	Reason two	Reason three

Structure

An **opinion piece** has a rather loose and flexible structure. However, like many persuasive texts, they feature an **introductory paragraph**, **body paragraphs** and **concluding paragraph**.

Introductory paragraph

The opening paragraph of an opinion piece may **outline the topic or main ideas**, but it may also just hint at these. Usually it will be easy to identify the writer's attitude towards the focus topic. The introduction will also give a sense of the writer's **passion** for the topic, as well as show that he or she is fiercely opposed to contrary positions.

Activity 1

Carefully read the sample **introduction** below and then answer the questions below.

What are we? Rats? Do we want to be eating cardboard and random pieces of plastic for dinner? Of course we don't, well, at least not consciously anyway. Yet so many people are—unconsciously—consuming food that is essentially non-food. Genetically modified food is **not** food. Food is naturally occurring and made by nature, not made by a person in a lab coat holding a beaker.

a What do you think the **topic** of this opinion piece is?

____

____

b What is the writer's **attitude** to this topic?

____

____

c What is the **position** that the writer **opposes**?

____

____

Activity 2

Below are some notes that a student has written when planning an opinion piece about pop music. Read through them carefully.

Pop music

- mindlessly repetitive beats and melodies
- meaningless lyrics, often misogynistic or sexual in content
- voices are modified heavily by technology, especially Auto-Tune
- many pop artists, such as Toni Braxton, Meatloaf and Billy Joel, have had to declare bankruptcy due to mismanagement of finances by managers.

What do you think will be the writer's **thesis statement** about pop music? Write it on the lines below. Remember that a thesis statement is the main argument about a topic and should be interesting.

Activity 3

Use your notes from the planning stage to begin drafting the **introductory paragraph** of your opinion piece on climate change. Use your own paper for this.

Body paragraphs

The **body paragraphs** of an opinion piece tend to be less structured than those of other persuasive texts. This is because the writer is driven by his or her passion for the topic and may get carried away by this passion, resulting in paragraphs where one point might lead into another in an unstructured way. However, some paragraphs may be very tightly structured and make concise, logical arguments.

The nature of an opinion piece is that it fiercely adheres to **one side of an issue** and aggressively attacks the ideas relating to the opposing position. It is this **biased nature** that distinguishes it from an argument essay which is much more balanced. Within the body paragraphs you must **passionately defend** your position. Give **examples** from current events, news reports, research articles and your personal experience to support your ideas.

Activity 4

Below is an example of a tightly structured and logical **body paragraph** from an opinion piece (polemic) answering the question *Is science good?*

This evidence does not serve to fully answer the question about science's contribution to human welfare, but it provides a pretty powerful example. One could very credibly expand on this evidence and argue that the modern Western lifespan has increased by 20 or so years since the industrial revolution through the scientific discovery of germ theory – responsible for not just vaccines but also antiseptic surgery, antibiotics and modern sanitation practices. I am not sure how one would estimate the number of lives this achievement has saved over the past century and a half, but it's almost certainly in the hundreds of millions.

Source: www.socialpolemics.com/2013/10/07/is-science-good

Read the paragraph closely and then answer the questions below.

a What is the **topic** of this opinion piece?

b What is the writer's **attitude** towards this topic?

c Find an example of where the writer's opinion and **passion** is shown.

d What **evidence** does the writer use to support his or her opinion?

Activity 5

Read the two **body paragraphs** about veganism below.

Example One

Suppose everyone in the world voluntarily stopped eating meat, en masse. If this collective change of spirit came to pass what would the ramifications be? I know it's not actually going to happen. But the best-case scenario from a climate perspective would be if all seven billion of us woke up one day and realised that the vegans were right all along.

Example Two

Veganism is the decision to refrain from consuming, or using in any form, animal products. The term originated in the 1940s and many people claim that their decision is prompted by ethical concerns. Vegans are difficult to cater for when they come over for dinner.

Identify which paragraph fits more with the style of an opinion piece: strength of feeling, appropriate content and ability to convince. Briefly explain your choice using the given space.

Activity 6

Write one of the **body paragraphs** of your opinion piece on climate change. Use your own paper for this.

Concluding paragraph

The **concluding paragraph** of an opinion piece nearly always leaves the reader wanting to continue reading, or to start asking questions or challenging the writer's opinions. If this is the response someone has after reading your polemic, then you know you have written a great, **provocative** piece.

Activity 7

Below is an example of a well-written **concluding paragraph**. Do you agree or disagree with the opinion? Circle which position you choose and then use the space below to list points justifying whether you agree or disagree.

It upsets me that one day I will need to spend hours of potential playtime 'media-educating' my sons about how stereotypical and exploitative representations of women are in advertising, video games, film and television. There are days when I am thankful that I did not have a daughter, for fear that she might have fallen prey to the marketing aimed at young girls, encouraging them to accept sexualised notions of femininity as being normal. Could we one day live in a world that does not have these gross misrepresentations of gender? I wish I could say we will, but I lack hope.

Agree **Disagree**

Activity 8

Write two sentences to express what you want your readers to think or do after reading the **concluding paragraph** to your opinion piece on the climate change topic.

a

b

Activity 9

It's now time for you to draft the **concluding paragraph** to your opinion piece on the climate change topic. Use your own paper for this.

Language feature

Sentence types

There are **three main sentence types** and a good persuasive writer will use all three in their opinion piece. Using a variety of sentence types will help you to create mood, pace and engage your reader.

The three main sentence types are:

- **simple**
- **compound**
- **complex**.

Simple sentences

These are sentences containing **one independent clause**, which has one subject and one verb.

subject verb
For example: The scientists tested the air.

Compound sentences

These are sentences containing **two independent clauses** joined by a conjunction.

subject verb subject verb
For example: The people were outraged and they protested in the streets.
↑
conjunction

Complex sentences

These are sentences with **at least one independent clause** with **one or more dependent clauses**.

For example: I asked for clarification many times but the people on the phone, who I assumed to be well educated, refused to assist me in my enquiries.

Other types of sentences that are used in opinion pieces include:

- **questions** (e.g. Why do we continue to ignore this issue?)
- **commands** (e.g. You must stop supporting factory farming.)
- **exclamations** (e.g. The issue drives me to the brink of insanity!)
- **statements** (e.g. The future is bleak.)

Activity 1

Turn each pair of sentences into a **compound** or **complex sentence** by adding the appropriate **conjunction** from the list below.

because	and	so	as	yet	while

a People have no interest in sustainability. It might negatively impact their lifestyles.

b The earth is warming at alarming rates. No one is doing anything.

c Parents must work at becoming healthier. They will be more active for their children.

d The number of female coders is dropping. The demand for coders is soaring.

e Children enjoy playing outside. They love playing in the open.

f Volunteering is easy. Many people do it regularly.

Activity 2

Change these statements/questions/commands/exclamations to the **type of sentence** given in brackets.

a They're a showcase for new possibilities. (question)

b She declared herself a master mapmaker. (exclamation)

c The game has five missions to complete. (command)

d We won! (question)

e Would you like to support our project? (command)

f I love this idea! (question)

Activity 3

Match the **sentence type** with the appropriate example.

a I don't disagree with them either.	question
b We must act now!	statement
c I believe there are serious flaws in the way we think about refugees.	exclamation
d Argue forcefully.	command
e What can we do to stop young people eating unhealthy food?	exclamation
f That's disgusting!	statement
g We love to celebrate the gifts of all young people!	question
h Will religion and science ever coexist?	exclamation

Spotlight on spelling

Homographs

Homographs are pairs of words that are **spelt the same way**, yet have quite **different meanings**. The two words may be pronounced the same way or differently. There are many homographs in the English language, and knowing some of the main ones will help you achieve spelling success.

For example:

compound: mix or combine
compound: an enclosed area that contains buildings
compound: make something more complex

content: happy or satisfied
content: something contained within something else (e.g. book content)

wound: past tense of verb *wind*, meaning 'wrap around' (e.g. wind the clock)
wound: an injury

Homophones

Homophones are pairs of words that are **pronounced the same way**, but are spelt differently and have different meanings.

For example:

pair: two similar or identical things that are matched
pear: an edible fruit

paws: the feet of an animal
pause: a temporary stop or rest

band: a group of instrumentalists
banned: prohibited or forbidden

Activity 1

Use a dictionary to define the **homograph** pairs below. The part of the word that is stressed when spoken has been underlined.

a object/object ______________________________

____

b produce/produce ______________________________

____

c minute/minute ______________________________

____

d frequent/frequent ______________________________

____

e desert/desert ______________________________

____

f entrance/entrance ______________________________

____

g moped/moped ______________________________

____

Activity 2

Use a dictionary to define the following pairs of **homophones**.

a insight/incite

___

___

c cite/sight

___

___

d taut/taught

___

___

e manner/manor

___

___

Activity 3

Circle the correct word in each sentence below. You may need to use a dictionary to help with some of these **homophones**.

a It concerns me that our politicians don't have the (presence/presents) of mind to ask their constituents what matters to them.

b The main (principal/principle) that must be understood here is that of justice.

c Of (coarse/course) we must take into consideration the feelings of the original inhabitants of this land before we make any concrete decisions.

d There is nothing more (intense/intents) than the awareness that you are being judged by your gender, rather than your brains.

e If you haven't already (guessed/guest), I'm not in favour of dredging The Great Barrier Reef.

f The most complicated (piece/peace) of this puzzle is the role that young people play.

g Under no circumstances should children be (allowed/aloud) to play R-rated video games.

You be the teacher

Below is a **body paragraph** for an opinion piece written by a Year 9 student. There are some errors in the structure of the paragraph and the spelling of some of the homophones. Can you correct the mistakes? Rewrite the paragraph with the **correct structure** and with the **correct spelling of all homophones**.

The death of all passenger vehicles wood be the lifeline our world desperately needs. It's a fact that cars are killing the planet. They really are. Those loud, smelly metallic monsters eat up our land and eat up the ozone layer. Our country's obsession with cars has got to end, or else we will fined ourselves living in a land of tar end fog. I truly believe that all cars should be band. It's disgusting. In Australia the number of passenger vehicles per 1000 people has increased from 153 in 1955 to 695 today.

Now you write

It is now time for you to complete your own **opinion piece** on climate change.

1 Before you write, take some time to look at the student writing sample on the following page as a guide to writing standards.

2 Once you have read the student writing sample, take some time to think about what you believe are the most important features of an opinion piece that you need to master.
Use the lines below to jot down your answer to this question:
What do you find most difficult when writing this kind of text?

3 Now look at the persuasive text marking criteria on page vi to double-check that you understand the requirements for a really good piece of persuasive writing.

Remember that you have already done your planning and drafted your introductory paragraph, one body paragraph and concluding paragraph. Use your own paper. Good luck!

Looking at other students' writing

Write an opinion piece addressing the question below:
Will genetically modified food save mankind?

Introduction
The introduction immediately alerts audience to the topic of the opinion piece: genetically modified food.

Rhetorical questions engage the reader.

Persuasive techniques
The student uses many modal words to show certainty and enforce point of view. The first person is used to show the student's personal opinion on the topic. Emotive words reinforce the student's position.

Text structure
The student uses the correct structure of an opinion piece including introduction, supporting paragraphs and conclusion.

Paragraphing
Each paragraph features one basic reason to support the student's point of view and evidence to support this reason. Some paragraphs are loosely structured, focusing more on opinion than evidence.

ADVANCED SAMPLE

WILL GENETICALLY MODIFIED FOOD SAVE MANKIND?

What are we? Rats? Do we want to be eating cardboard and random pieces of plastic for dinner? Of course we don't, well, at least not consciously anyway. Yet so many people are unconsciously consuming food that is essentially non-food. Genetically modified food is NOT food. Food is naturally occurring and made by nature, not made by a person in a lab coat holding a beaker.

Genetically modified food is food that has been modified in a way that does not occur in nature. People who support GMOs (genetically modified organisms) argue that this process will improve the amount of food we can grow, because crops can be created to be resistant to disease and pests. This may be true, but the consequences of playing around with nature will be profound!

Have these scientists never read the novel *Frankenstein*? What if some genetically modified food escapes into a wild population and a mutation grows as a result? No scientist can tell us what the result of this would be. Therefore we should not be exploring genetically modified foods as an option to sustain mankind.

Ecofarming is the perfect alternative to GMOs. This type of farming sees farmers respecting their natural environment, not polluting it with synthetic fertilisers, toxic chemicals and potentially harmful GMOs. These farmers work hard to protect the soil and water and promote biodiversity. Through their efforts, humanity will be saved.

We all know science is impressive, yet I continue to be surprised by the failure of scientists and politicians to take notice of failed experiments such as the cane toads in Queensland. We should be protecting the wonderful world we have, not trying to invent an unnatural future.

Vocabulary
Language choices are appropriate to the student's purpose—to persuade people to think critically about genetically modified food. Complex and precise words are used to talk about the topic.

Sentence structure
All sentences are grammatically correct, well structured and meaningful and use a variety of sentence patterns.

Ideas
Ideas are well selected and relevant with a lot of detail to support the student's position that genetically modified food will not save mankind.

Cohesion
The student uses pronouns to create connections within paragraphs (e.g. *these* and *it*).

Punctuation
Correct punctuation is used throughout the opinion piece.

Spelling
All words are correctly spelt.

UNIT THREE

Persuasive texts

Television advertisement scripts

Understanding the question

Script a television advertisement for a new brand of dog food.

Type of question

This question is asking you to write a particular type of persuasive text—a **television advertisement**.

A television advertisement requires you to persuade viewers to **purchase a particular product or service**. In this question you are being asked to persuade viewers to purchase a new brand of dog food.

The word **script** tells you that you do not have to film the advertisement; you just need to write the script that would be used to film it.

Features of a television advertisement script

- Aims to persuade people to purchase a product or change their behaviour
- Has a loose three-part structure intended to catch the viewer's attention, explain the product and repeat key ideas
- Includes descriptions of audio and visual information such as sound effects, voice overs and images to be shown on screen
- Uses persuasive, subjective and even biased language
- Often features language devices such as exaggeration, juxtaposition and puns
- Written in present tense

1 The word **script** can be used as a noun and a verb. Define each below.

script (noun) ______________________________

____

script (verb) ______________________________

____

2 Identify five television advertisements that have convinced you to try a new product or service.

____

____

3 Below is a list of popular dog foods in Australia. Put a tick beside the ones you have heard of.

a Pal ☐

b Advance ☐

c Pedigree ☐

d Purina ☐

e Chum ☐

Planning and organisation

You have been asked to advertise a new brand of dog food. This will require some critical and creative thinking. First, **brainstorm** the **features** of the new brand of dog food. Then you need to imagine ways that this dog food is **different** from other dog foods. For example, does it have extra vitamins, more protein, bigger serves, extra vegetables, or is it scientifically formulated?

TIP The average television advertisement only lasts 30 seconds. This means that you must do some serious planning if you're going to fit all the necessary information into such a short space!

Activity 1

Use the spider-map below to **brainstorm** all of the **special features** that your dog food has. An example has been done for you.

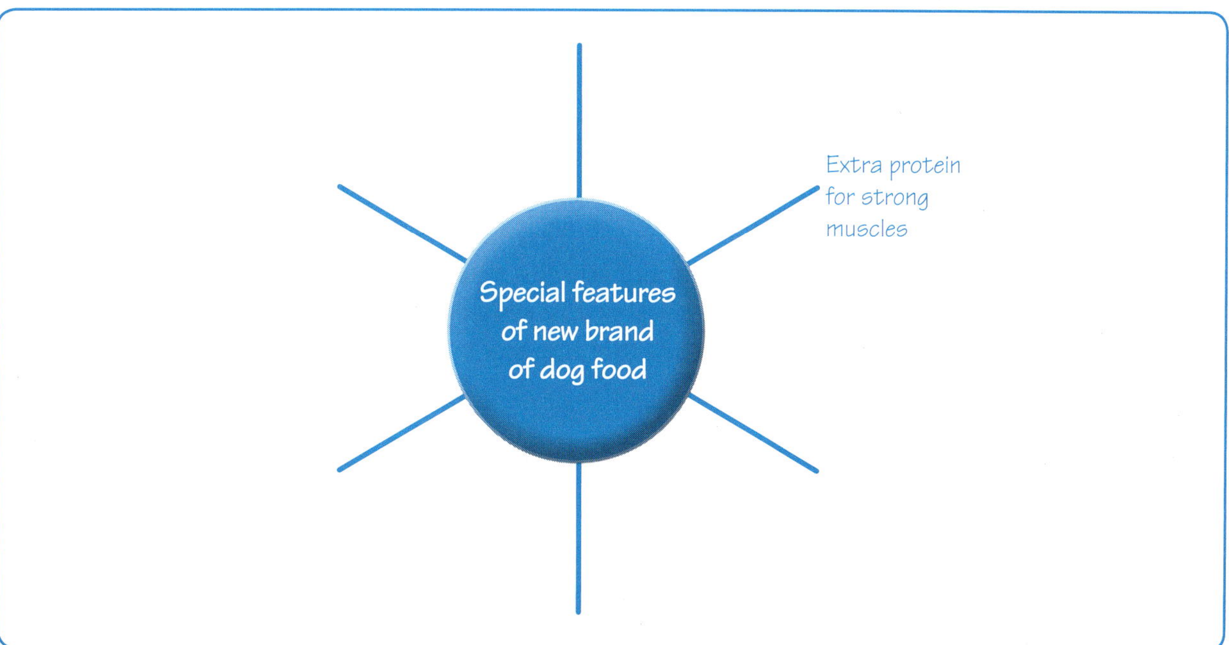

Activity 2

The next stage requires you to think critically. Use the internet to watch other dog food advertisements. Take notes on the **features of the advertisements** and write them in the table below. If you can't watch an advertisement, think about what might be the features of dog food advertisements. You have probably seen some TV advertisements for dog food so use this experience to help you.

Descriptions of dog food	Images shown on screen
Types of voice(s) heard	**Promised benefits of dog food**

3 Now it's time to write a brief **plan** for your dog food advertisement. On your own paper, write some notes about the following elements of your television advertisement:

- images on screen
- types of voices heard
- product benefits
- descriptions of the product.

Structure

The purpose of a television advertisement is first to **hook the viewer's interest** and, second, to **convince** them that they need to purchase the product being advertised. With this purpose in mind, most advertisements use a three-part structure. They:

- identify the product with a **lead sentence**
- explain the **best features** of the product, and
- **repeat the main idea** from the lead sentence in a concluding sentence.

Lead sentence

This is essentially one or two sentences that establish the **mood** of your commercial and **grab the attention** of your viewer. The very first sentence should relate exactly to what you are advertising. For this writing task, that is a new brand of dog food.

The introduction to a television commercial must do three things:

- **attract** the viewer's attention
- use a voice and style that will immediately **engage** the target audience
- leave the viewer **wanting to know more** about the product.

  For example: Welcome to Mount Hellier's Hotel, where you'll be treated like royalty and sleep like a baby.

Activity 1

Below are two sentences for **television advertisements**. For each one, answer the following two questions.

a What product or service is being advertised?

b Which words or phrases make the product or service sound appealing to you?

i Luscious, plump fruits and crunchy, crisp muesli make the perfect breakfast combination.

a ______________________________

____

b ______________________________

____

____

ii All the pop songs you love to sing along to, brought together in one compilation.

a ____

____

b ____

____

Activity 2

Match the **lead sentences** to their products.

a Crispy roasted peanuts, covered in silky smooth caramel.	sports car
b Tired of flat, lifeless locks?	chocolate bar
c There's no time to go slow in today's fast-paced world.	shampoo
d Talk, text and tweet all you want!	car insurance
e Accidents do happen, but no one wants to get caught with the bill!	mobile phone plan

Activity 3

Write the **lead sentence** for your **television advertisement** of a new brand of dog food.

____

____

____

____

____

Product explanation

Once you have your viewers hooked, the middle section of a television advertisement must provide them with **further information** about the product. This may include any of the following:

- special features
- who the product is suitable for
- price
- benefits of this product.

There are many different ways that these details can be communicated to viewers. Here are some of the most common **strategies** that advertisements use to convince viewers to buy a product:

- celebrity **endorsement**
- **appeal to vanity** (suggesting you will be a better person if you buy the product)
- **testimonials** from everyday people
- **guilt** (trying to make you feel bad if you don't purchase the product).

Activity 4

Look at the list of products given below. Identify which **strategy** you think would be best to sell each of the products. Explain your reason for each selection.

a perfume

____

b dishwashing detergent

____

c vitamins for children

____

d moisturiser

____

For this section of the advertisement, it is important to decide who will be **speaking** (voice-over, actors, celebrities, everyday people), what they will be saying and what **images** will be displayed on screen when they are speaking. It's a good idea to consider what **sound effects or music** will be used in your advertisement as well.

Read the example television advertisement script below to see how the audio and visual is laid out.

Product: Choco (chocolate and malt powder)

VIDEO	AUDIO
Child jumping on trampoline.	Child: Hey Mum, I'm starving!
Mum sitting on chair on balcony, reading.	Mum: *(sighs)*
Shot of Choco being stirred into a glass of milk.	Voice-over: Children use up a lot of energy through play and it's not always easy keeping them fuelled for play. Why not give them a glass of Choco?
Child smiling with glass of Choco in hand.	Child: Chocolate milk? Yum!
Mum speaking to the camera.	Mum: *(to the camera)* And he doesn't even know it's good for him.
Shot of Choco tin and empty glass.	Voice-over: Keep your kids ready for play all day. Give them a Choco.

Activity 5

Match the **audio** to the **video** in the table below.

a Keeping in touch is simple with the Nikita 320.	children playing in a front yard
b Clean fresh breath and shiny white teeth.	a girl on her phone
c You want an active, healthy dog.	a man brushing his teeth
d The perfect family home is waiting for you at Moore Gardens.	a dog catching a frisbee

Activity 6

Here are a student's notes for the **voice-over** of a television advertisement for a perfume.

Wear 'Flowers' by Renata.
There's nothing purer than the smell of fresh flowers.
Make a statement.
A hint of jasmine, a touch of jonquil, a mix of lavender.

Complete the tasks based on these notes above.

a The sentences are jumbled. Rewrite the lines so they make sense. Use the lines provided for this.

b What do you think the **video** would be to accompany the words? Write your answers in note form.

Activity 7

Draft the **product explanation** for your dog food advertisement. Make sure you include both **audio** and **visual** components. Use your own paper for this activity.

Concluding sentence

The purpose of the end of a television advertisement is to **reinforce its main message** and to force the viewer to act. It may want people to buy a certain product, to donate money or to change their opinions or behaviour in some way. The most effective method of getting people to act is through **repetition of main ideas** and giving **commands**. You may wish to repeat all or part of your lead sentence to remind the viewers of the product.

For example: So, do yourself a favour and spend the night at Mount Hellier's Hotel, where your comfort matters.

Activity 8

Draft the **concluding sentence** for your dog food television advertisement. Don't forget to describe the **video** to be seen by viewers.

Language feature

Juxtaposition

This is a **literary device** where two characters, objects, actions or ideas are placed **side by side** for the purpose of **exaggerating differences**. Often juxtaposition is used in advertising to show the difference between two products. The intention can be to surprise or shock viewers, and make them think more positively about the product being advertised as it is always shown to be the better of the two.

It is important to note that, for legal reasons, the writer cannot mention the brand name of other products. The writer can carefully hint or speak broadly of 'other hair products' (for example) but can't name them.

Activity 1

Complete each **juxtaposition** with the correct product from the box. The first one has been done for you.

washing detergent	hair gel	laptop	digital watch	school shoes

a Sick of clothes that smell like lady's perfume? You need Man-Made *washing detergent*.

b Other brands leave you feeling like you are wearing a motorcycle helmet, but not Tough Nut ____________________.

c Shoe polish is a thing of the past when you wear Darkus ____________________.

d No need for pockets or expensive phone holders when you have a Wrapt ____________________.

e Snail-paced booting up is a thing of the past when you get an Asis2140 ____________________.

Activity 2

Below is a list of branded products. Write a sentence that **juxtaposes** them with a similar branded product to **exaggerate their differences**. The first one has been done for you.

a Cheetah sports shoes

Some sports shoes look good; ours ARE good.

b Maxi Chocolate Bar

____

____

c Brown's Potato Chips

____

____

d Bare Fruit Juice

____

____

Language feature

Puns

Humour is a common technique used by advertisers to engage viewers. One popular way to create humour in advertisements is to use a **pun**.

A pun is a **deliberate play on words** which has an intentional humorous effect. Puns are typically made by misusing homophones or homonyms, or by using a word which has two different meanings.

Examples of common puns:
An elephant's opinion carries a lot of weight.
A horse is a very stable animal.
Time flies like an arrow. Fruit flies like a banana.

Example of an advertising pun: It's how the smooth take the rough. (Range Rover)

In this example above, the word *smooth* is used to refer to the character of the people who buy Range Rovers—meaning they are refined and classy.

A pun will typically be used in a lead sentence or in the concluding sentence of an advertisement.

Some famous examples of puns in advertisements include:
Toyota: *The car in front is a Toyota.*
Vitamin Water: *Amaze-zinc*
Tic Tacs: *Tic Tac. Surely the best tactic.*

Activity 3

In the **puns** below, underline the words that have been intentionally used to create a **humorous effect** and then briefly explain why each pun is funny. The first one has been done for you.

a The dead batteries were given out free of charge.

The word *charge* has a double meaning in this pun. It refers to cost and electrical power. It is funny because dead batteries have no electrical power.

b What do you get from a pampered cow? Spoiled milk.

c When a clock is hungry it goes back four seconds.

d When she told me I was average, she was just being mean.

e I used to hate maths but then I realised decimals have a point.

Activity 4

Below is a list of **homophones**. Use them to write a **pun** for the given product in brackets.

a sole/soul (a shoe shop)

b roar/raw (sushi restaurant)

c flaw/floor (flooring company)

d use/ewes (knitted jumper)

Spotlight *on spelling*

The letters *c* and *g* can be pronounced in two different ways.

Hard and soft *c*

If the letter *c* is followed by the vowel sounds *e*, *i* or *y*, then the pronunciation is soft.

For example: cider, citizen, cymbal, celery

There are some exceptions.

For example: soccer, Celt

If the letter *c* is followed by any letter other than those three, the pronunciation is hard.

For example: coin, cold, curse, cause

Hard and soft *g*

If the letter *g* is followed by the vowel sounds *e*, *i* or *y*, then the pronunciation is soft.

For example: digital, engine, gypsy, page

There are some exceptions.

For example: gear, get, girl, give

If the letter *g* is followed by any letter other than those three, the pronunciation is hard.

For example: goose, guest, regular, gain

Activity 1

Identify if the letter *c* is **hard** or **soft** in the words below. Write *H* for hard and *S* for soft.

a citrus ________	**b** cupid ________	**c** civil ________
d dance ________	**e** bouncy ________	**f** cease ________
g carry ________	**h** code ________	

Activity 2

Identify if the letter *g* is **hard** or **soft** in the words below. Write *H* or *S* on the lines.

a gas ________	**b** guide ________	**c** guard ________
d good ________	**e** energy ________	**f** allergy ________
g original ________	**h** gentle ________	

You be the teacher

Below is part of a **television advertisement script** written by a Year 9 student. There are some errors in the structure of the script and the spelling of some of the words. Can you correct the mistakes? Rewrite the paragraph with the **correct structure** and with the **correct spelling of all words**.

The course is only 8 km, making it perfect for the entire family. Rejister now to get the discounted early-bird rates and selebrate summer with a bit of healthy kompetition. Sun, surf and fitness! A mid-week event, the Manly-to-the-Spit short race attrakts up to 3000 people annually.

____

____

____

____

Now you write

It is now time for you to complete your own **script for a television advertisement** for a brand-new dog food.

1. Before you write, take some time to look at the student writing sample on the following page as a guide to writing standards.
2. Once you have read the student writing sample, take some time to think about what you believe are the most important features of a television advertisement that you need to master. Use your own paper to jot down your answer to this question:
   What do you find most difficult when writing this kind of text?
3. Now look at the persuasive text marking criteria on page vi to double-check that you understand the requirements for a really good piece of persuasive writing.

   Remember that you have already done your planning and drafted your lead sentence, product explanation and concluding sentence. Use your own paper. Good luck!

Looking at other students' writing

Write a script on the question below:

Write a television advertisement script for a new toothpaste.

Text structure
The student uses the correct structure of a television advertisement script: lead sentence, product explanation and conclusion. The advertisement also features description of visuals.

Paragraphing
The script is effectively divided into scenes, with each focusing on a feature of the product.

Ideas
Well-selected and relevant ideas with a lot of detail are used to convince viewers to buy the product. Humour is well used.

ADVANCED SAMPLE

TELEVISION ADVERTISEMENT SCRIPT FOR A NEW TOOTHPASTE

VIDEO	AUDIO
Woman creeps into her office cubicle after lunch and is handcuffed by 'Bad Breath Police'.	Don't get caught with bad breath. Arm yourself with new spearmint-flavoured Dentamint toothpaste.
Shot of woman from behind, putting Dentamint on her toothbrush.	Dentamint specially formulated toothpaste works all day long to ensure your breath is fresh and your smile is bright.
Woman throws the old brand of toothpaste in the bin.	Other toothpaste brands claim to keep your smile clean all day, but Dentamint actually does!
Woman walks confidently into her office cubicle after lunch, 'Bad Breath Police' stand aside, smiling, and let her sit down.	Remember: people who brush with Dentamint always have a clean record.

Introduction
The lead sentence grabs the viewers' attention and encourages them to want to know more about the product.

Vocabulary
Language choices are appropriate for the purpose of persuading people to buy the product. Precise words are used to talk about the topic.

Persuasive techniques
The student uses the second person *you* to engage the viewer with the product's features. Juxtaposition between brands reinforces the superiority of Dentamint. The pun *clean record* is amusing.

Spelling
All words are correctly spelt.

Punctuation
Correct punctuation is used throughout the script.

Cohesion
Repetition of the brand name and the product's benefits ensures cohesion.

Sentence structure
All sentences are grammatically correct, well structured and meaningful.

UNIT FOUR

Persuasive texts
Proposals

Understanding the question

Propose one innovative solution to littering in public spaces for a submission to your local council.

Type of question

This question is asking you to write a particular type of persuasive text—a **proposal**.

How do you know it is a proposal that is required? The word *propose* is the clue—*proposal* is the noun from the verb *propose*. The word *propose* shows you are required to recommend or suggest a **solution to a problem**. Here, you are being asked to propose an innovative solution to littering in public. Littering in public is the identified problem that you will attempt to solve.

Features of a proposal

- Aims to convince an interested party to commit to a project or begin a professional partnership with the person presenting the proposal
- Presents a solution to a particular problem or presents ideas for a future project
- Should be highly engaging
- Has a clear structure to provide the audience with a clear understanding of the proposed project or solution
- Can be spoken or written
- Consists of succinct paragraphs
- Persuasive and passionate language is supported by factual evidence, such as statistics, quotes or data

1 Circle words from the list below which are **synonyms** for the word propose.

offer claim provoke suggest recommend

2 Define the following **content words** as used in the question.

a innovative ____________________

____

b solution ____________________

____

c littering ____________________

____

d public ____________________

____

Planning and organisation

Activity 1

The first thing to do when confronted with a problem to solve is to brainstorm what you already know. On the two spider-maps below, **brainstorm** everything you know about the reasons why people litter in public spaces, and the personal and environmental consequences of littering.

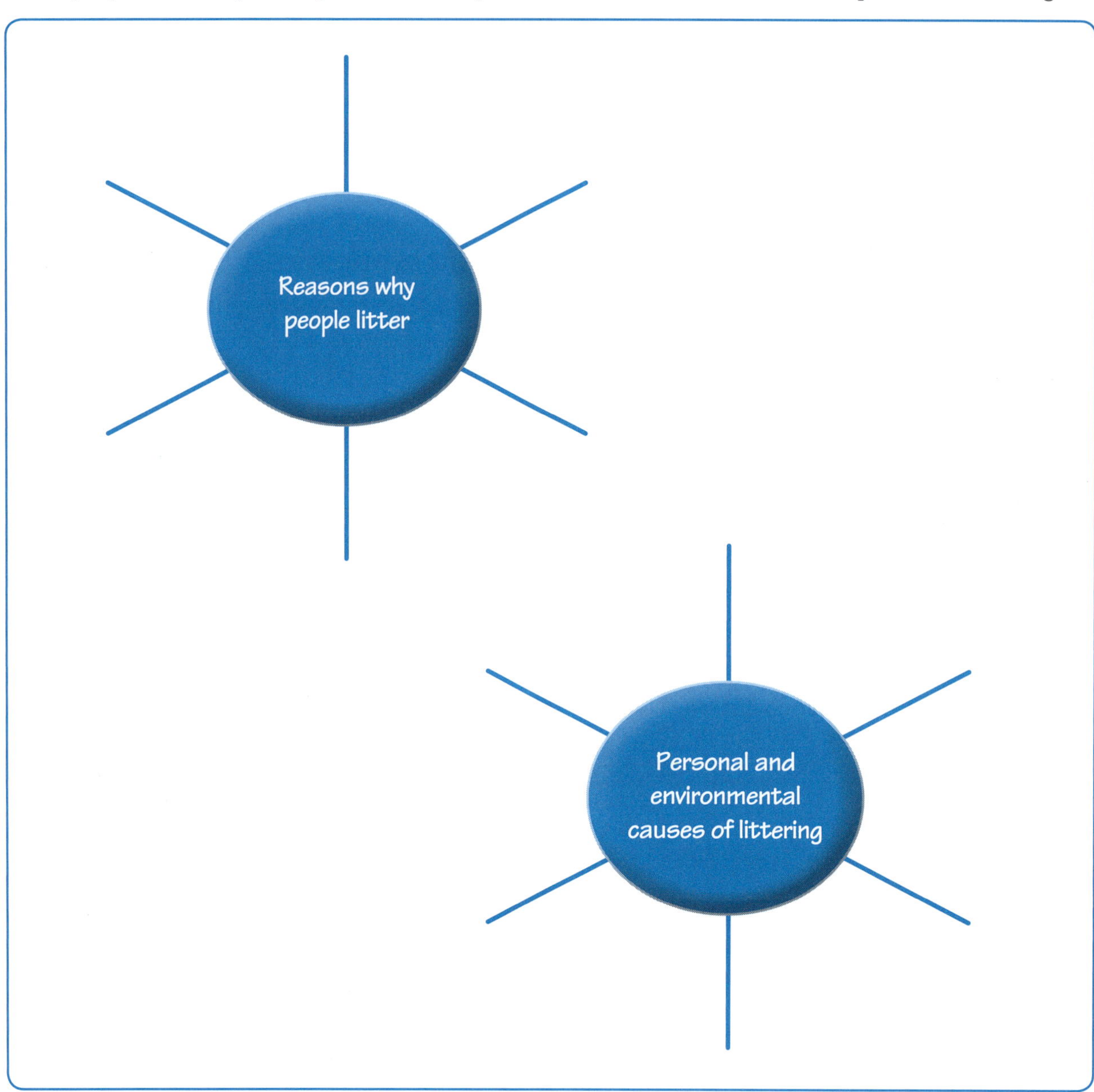

Activity 2

Choose two **consequences** of littering that you think will be the most effective in convincing people to solve this problem. Write them on the lines below.

Activity 3

Choose three **causes** of public littering from your brainstorming above. In the table below, list as many **solutions** as you can think of for each cause of littering. This is a free-thinking activity, so come up with as many wacky ideas as possible. The purpose of this task is to generate a lot of ideas and from those, select the ones you think will be the most effective.

Cause 1	Cause 2	Cause 3
Solutions	**Solutions**	**Solutions**

Activity 4

Read through all of your ideas. It is now time to select the idea that you think is the most innovative and effective to solve the problem of people littering in public spaces. In the box below, summarise your proposed **solution** in three to five points.

My solution to littering

Structure

Writing a proposal requires a careful balance of **persuasion** and **information**. You need to be persuasive so you can convince your audience to accept your proposal but you also need to be informative so they understand why your proposed solution will be effective.

The general structure of a proposal includes:

* a **problem** statement
* project **goals** and suggested **strategies**
* an **overview** of expected **results**.

Problem statement

The opening paragraph of your proposal will identify a problem and argue in favour of implementing a project to solve this problem. This paragraph should include:

* a brief description of the **identified problem**—including causes and consequences
* a brief **explanation** of why this problem needs to be solved
* **evidence**—such as quotes, research data, descriptions or photographs—to support your argument regarding the identified problem.

The language in this paragraph should be highly **persuasive** and use a serious and urgent tone.

Activity 1

Read the sample **problem statement** below and identify the following elements. Simply write *a*, *b* or *c* near the element.

a a brief description of the **identified problem**

b a brief **explanation** of why this problem needs to be solved

c use of **evidence** to support the argument regarding the identified problem

Skateboard riders do not have enough safe, purposely designated spaces to ride in our council area. As a result, skaters are often riding in public spaces, including roads, and being seen as a nuisance by the general public. Without a designated space, skaters are at risk of being hit by cars or involved in disputes with non-skaters. There are many underutilised public spaces, such as under bridges, that could be easily converted into skate bowls to accommodate the needs of skaters. Such an innovative solution has had great success in other suburban areas, including suburbs in Brisbane and Melbourne.

Activity 2

Below are sentences from a **problem statement** written by a Year 9 student. They are out of order. Number them from 1 to 3 to show the correct sequence.

_____ This invasive species preys on small birds and marsupials, with over 35 species of birds and 36 species of mammals identified as being at threat.

_____ Australian native wildlife is under threat from an introduced predator—the feral cat.

_____ Failure to introduce measures to reduce the number of feral cats will have catastrophic consequences for our native wildlife.

Activity 3

Write the **problem statement** for your solution to the littering problem.

Project goals and suggested strategies

This is the most important part of the proposal. It is usually about two or three paragraphs in length. This is where you outline the **goals** of your proposed action or project, and how you aim to achieve these goals through your innovative **strategies**.

Of course, you need to create realistic goals and that means establishing **measurable, achievable objectives**. In order to do this, ask yourself the questions below.

* What are my long-term goals?
* What are my short-term goals? What strategies will I use to achieve these?
* What are some challenges or obstacles I might face?
* What parameters (limitations) can I put on my project in order for it to be feasible? Place and time are important parameters to consider.

The project goals section will begin with a **strong project goal sentence**.

For example: This project aims to improve the level of grain production in the region by 10% by the end of 2015.

Activity 4

Below is a student's first draft of a **goal sentence** for a proposal to reduce the voting age from 18 to 16. Rewrite the sentence so it has more measurable and achievable goals and is expressed more forcefully. Remember to consider both short- and long-term goals and/or parameters.

We think that we believe that young people should get a chance to have a say and we want them to be able to vote.

Activity 5

Think about your littering **proposal** task and answer the planning questions below.

a What are my long-term goals?

b What are my short-term goals?

c What parameters can I put on my project in order for it to be feasible?

d What are some challenges or obstacles I might face?

Activity 6

Write the **project goal sentence** for your littering proposal. Use your own paper for this.

Next you need to outline the **strategies** that you suggest will achieve your goal.

For example, a strategy to encourage young people to attend events run by the local youth council might be to raise awareness of upcoming events. Activities to support this strategy might be having youth workers speak at school assemblies or putting advertising posters up in schools.

Try to give specific examples of activities that you would want to implement in order to support your strategy.

Activity 7

Below is a list of proposal goals created by young people. For each one, identify a potential **strategy** to help achieve these goals.

a Our project aims to reduce the amount of packaged food eaten by young people aged 12 to 18.

____

b This project hopes to reduce rates of cyberbullying amongst Greentree High School students by 20% in the next five years.

____

c We wish to raise awareness of the harmful effects that factory farming has on pigs in the Hunter region.

____

d Our goal is to bring about an end to trolleys being left in the car park of the shopping centre at Warriewood.

____

Activity 8

It's now time to draft the **paragraphs** outlining your **project goals and strategies**. Make sure you read back through your planning to help with this task. Use your own paper.

Overview of expected results

This is your final opportunity to convince your audience to support your proposal, so make it count. There are two main components to discuss in this part of your proposal: **outcomes** and **impacts**.

Your job is to convince your audience that the solution you are proposing will have immediate outcomes for the stakeholders and will ultimately have a long-term impact on people's behaviour or attitudes. The paragraph ends with a powerful and emotive **call to action**.

Activity 9

Read the following example of an expected results paragraph and answer the questions below.

We firmly believe that the introduction of mandatory desexing of all male cats will significantly decrease the number of feral cats in Lane Cove National Park. By providing cat owners with a rebate for desexing their male cats, we predict an increase in the number of desexed cats in the first six months. Following this, the number of unwanted kittens will drop, leading in the long term to a reduced number of cats being dumped in the national park. The health and safety of our native fauna is at risk if we do not act now and implement this proposed solution to the growing feral cat population in Lane Cove National Park.

a What does the writer claim will be the **outcomes** of the proposal?

b What does the writer claim will be the **long-term impact** of the proposal?

c What is the **call to action** the writer includes?

Activity 10

Write the **expected results paragraph** for your proposal.

Language features

Metaphors and similes

Metaphors and similes are figures of speech used to provide a **comparison between two dissimilar ideas, objects or experiences**. The purpose of these devices is to better describe one thing by comparing it to another. They often help to **clarify** ideas or make a point in an argument. They can also **add impact** to a description.

A simile compares one thing to another with the use of the words *like* or *as*.

A metaphor says that one thing is another thing.

For example:
She sings like an angel. (simile)
Their icy relationship began to thaw. (metaphor)

When writing a proposal, using a simile or metaphor might help your listeners better understand or appreciate the problem that you are trying to solve.

Activity 1

Match the concept to the appropriate **metaphor**.

a Racism	**i** is a disease contracted by prolonged exposure to digital devices and the internet.
b Technology addiction	**ii** is a trap that the young fall into, which many find hard to claw their way out of.
c Poverty	**iii** can feel like an old wound reopened by the rough play of ignorance and injustice.
d Youth homelessness	**iv** can only be solved by bridging the gap between the rich and poor.

Activity 2

Choose the **metaphor** in each sentence pair below.

a Deforestation
- **i** The deforestation in South America is a cancer on the lungs of our planet.
- **ii** Deforestation is like cancer. It erodes soils, pollutes waterways and decreases biodiversity.

b Climate change
- **i** Climate change is the iceberg that will sink humanity's ship.
- **ii** Climate change is like a sinking ship. We need to do something about it now.

c Poor dietary habits of young people
- **i** Obesity is a plague that our youth are contracting via the advertising of unhealthy food and drinks.
- **ii** Advertising of unhealthy foods and drink is causing a plague. We propose a ban on all advertising.

Spotlight *on spelling*

i before *e* except after *c*

This is one of the first spelling rules you will memorise as a child. Why? Because it rhymes! Unfortunately, this rule is not as simple as it sounds. This is because there are quite a few exceptions to the rule, which sometimes makes it difficult to spell certain words. Below is an overview of the main rule, as well as a few of the more common exceptions to it that you will encounter.

It is true that ***i* comes before *e*** in most words we commonly use, but these are words **where the letter *e* has a long sound like *ee***.

For example: believe, niece, piece, siege, fierce

However, the letter *i* comes **after** *e* in long *ee* words **where both letters are preceded by a *c***.

For example: deceive, perceive, receive

There are a few other long *ee* words that do not follow the rule.

For example: either

The letter *i* comes **after** the letter *e* in words where **together** they create the **long *a* sound**.

For example: neighbour, surveillance, reign, veil, beige

The *i* before *e* rule except after *c* **doesn't apply to words from the Latin root *sci***.

For example: omniscient, conscience, prescient

Many other **words borrowed from foreign languages** don't follow the *i* before *e* rule either.

For example: caffeine, forfeit, heist, sovereign, foreign

Activity 1

Complete each word by writing either *ie* or *ei*.

a When young people travel to for_____gn lands they broaden their outlook.

b The feral cat will no longer r_____gn supreme in Lane Cove National Park.

c Upon rec_____pt of the latest data, we swiftly changed our project's direction.

d There is no time for l_____sure when we have a deadline to meet.

e Some people will think that our passion for sustainable seafood is w_____rd, but we don't care.

f You may have a loved one or a fr_____nd who suffers from undiagnosed depression.

g It is essential that we ach_____ve our goal of limiting game playing by 30%.

h The v_____l of ignorance of this issue must be lifted.

i The glass c_____ling is an issue that must be addressed in the 21st century.

j Research has found that over 50% of people do not know the name of their next-door n_____ghbour.

k We must s_____ze this opportunity to make a difference to the lives of Indigenous children.

Activity 2

Identify the **spelling errors** in the passage below. Write the correct spelling of all errors in the space provided.

Nieghbourhood Watch has been an Australian institution for decades. Unfortunately fewer and fewer people are participating in this worthwhile organisation, resulting in it being unable to acheive the goals of community cohesion and safety. Our proposed campaign, 'Freinds Everywhere', aims to reconnect individuals with thier nieghbours to establish supportive relationships. We firmly believe that this project will ensure that we do not forfiet the necessary social bonds first established by Neighbourhood Watch.

_____________________ _____________________

_____________________ _____________________

_____________________ _____________________

You be the teacher

Below is a **body paragraph** for a proposal written by a Year 9 student. There are some errors in the structure of the paragraph and the spelling of some words. Can you correct the mistakes? Rewrite the paragraph with the **correct structure** and with the **correct spelling of all words**.

The number one activity we plan to implement to support this strategy is the introduction of an afterschool fun club once a week. This club will help students discover thier creativity and encourage them to pursue non-digital activities in thier spare time. Our primary objective is to decrease the weekly incidence of cyberbullying in our school by the end of the year. Our main strategy to acheive this goal is to raise awareness of the positive benefits of spending more time away from screens. It is important that we act now to address the negative impact that cyberbullying is having on children in primary school. We firmly beleive that this will lead to a decrease in cyberbullying at our school.

Now you write

It is now time for you to complete your own **proposal** on the littering topic.

1 Before you write, take some time to look at the student writing sample on the following page as a guide to writing standards.

2 Once you have read the student writing sample, take some time to think about what you believe are the most important features of a proposal that you need to master. Use the lines below to jot down your answer to this question:
What do you find most difficult when writing this kind of text?

3 Now look at the persuasive text marking criteria on page vi to double-check that you understand the requirements for a really good piece of persuasive writing.

Remember that you have already done your planning and drafted your problem statement, project goals and suggested strategies, and overview of expected results. Use your own paper. Good luck!

Looking at other students' writing

Proposals:
Feral cats continue to kill wildlife in Greendale National Park. Propose an affordable solution to this problem.

ADVANCED SAMPLE

FERAL CATS CONTINUE TO KILL WILDLIFE IN GREENDALE NATIONAL PARK. PROPOSE AN AFFORDABLE SOLUTION TO THIS PROBLEM.

Australian native wildlife is under threat from the feral cat. This invasive species preys on small birds and marsupials, with over 35 species of birds and 36 species of mammals identified as being at threat. Failure to introduce measures to reduce the number of feral cats will have terrible consequences for our wildlife. We propose that mandatory desexing of all male cats will reduce the impact that feral cats have on the local native wildlife.

The long-term goal for this project is to increase the number of cats being desexed by 40% over the next five years. It is hoped that this will lead to a decrease in the number of feral cats and a decrease in the loss of native wildlife. Short-term goals for this project include speaking with local veterinarians in the Greendale area to introduce a rebate for people desexing male cats. A secondary goal is to promote this rebate to the population of the Greendale area.

In order to achieve our short-term goal of a rebate for desexing, we aim to visit all local veterinarians to deliver information packages about the proposed desexing rebate. These will inform the veterinarians of the benefits for them and for pet-owners in terms of cheaper desexing costs. Possible challenges for this strategy include veterinarians who do not want to participate, and the cost of the kits. Despite these, we believe this strategy will be effective.

Secondly, we will promote the campaign to the public via articles in the local newspaper, *The Greendale Daily*, and a flyer drop in mailboxes. We believe that both of these strategies will be effective as the newspaper has a wide readership, and flyers will promote savings to pet-owners. Obstacles to this strategy may include finding affordable printing and organising an interview with the local newspaper.

We firmly believe that the introduction of desexing of all male cats will decrease the number of feral cats in Greendale National Park. By providing cat owners with a rebate for desexing their male cats, we predict an increase in the number of desexed cats in the first six months. The health and safety of our native fauna is at risk if we do not act now and implement this proposed solution to the growing feral cat population in Greendale National Park.

Introduction
The introduction immediately alerts the audience to the nature of the proposal—a project aimed at lessening the impact of feral cats on native wildlife. Statistics are used effectively to support the proposed solution.

Persuasive techniques
Each paragraph outlines a specific aspect of the proposed solution, with a focus on strategies to ensure the solution is a success.

Text structure
The student uses the correct structure of a proposal including a problem statement, project goals and suggested strategies and an overview of expected results.

Paragraphing
Each paragraph features one basic reason to support the author's point of view and evidence to support this reason. The student effectively uses the SEW paragraph structure. The conclusion is strong and includes all required elements.

Vocabulary
Language choices are appropriate to the student's purpose—to propose a solution to feral cats killing wildlife. Complex and precise words are used to talk about the topic.

Sentence structure
All sentences are grammatically correct, well structured and meaningful, and use a variety of sentence patterns.

Ideas
Well-selected and relevant ideas with a lot of detail support the student's proposed solution to the problem.

Cohesion
Connecting words and pronouns such as *this* and *these* show clear connections between ideas.

Punctuation
Correct punctuation is used throughout the proposal.

Spelling
All words are correctly spelt.

UNIT FIVE

Informative texts
Critical analysis essays

Understanding the question

Write a critical analysis essay addressing the question below:

How does William Blake communicate ideas about childhood innocence in his poem 'The Chimney Sweeper'?

Type of question

This question is asking you to write a particular type of essay—a **critical analysis essay**.

How do you know a critical analysis essay is required and not another form of essay? The word *how* is the clue. It indicates that you are required to **explain and analyse** how literary techniques communicate ideas and emotions. Also, the reference to a literary text—the poem by William Blake—tells you that the topic of the essay is a **literary text**, in this case a poem.

You must develop a structured response that helps your reader better understand how Blake uses poetic devices to communicate ideas about childhood innocence in his poem. You must try to remember that the purpose of this essay type is to inform your reader.

Features of a critical analysis

- Aims to help your reader clearly understand how a text communicates ideas by analysing and evaluating a literary text
- Has a strict structure of an introduction, body and conclusion
- Supports ideas with evidence
- Includes evaluation of literary devices
- Uses third-person narrative and formal language

1 In your essay you will need to analyse **poetic devices** used by William Blake in his poem 'The Chimney Sweeper'. On the lines below, list any poetic devices you know.

2 The question you need to answer includes key **content words** that tell you what you must focus on in your essay. Write a brief definition of each of the content words.

a childhood innocence

b communicate

Planning and organisation

Before writing any critical analysis essay, you must do some **research**. The first item to research is the composer of the text. In this case, the composer is the poet William Blake.

Activity 1

Use library reference books or the internet to research information about Blake, and add that information to the table below.

a When he was born and died	
b Where he lived	
c Most well-known poem	
d Style of poetry	
e Celebrated for	

Activity 2

Read through the **poem** below. Read it to yourself first and then out loud.

The Chimney Sweeper

When my mother died I was very young,
And my father sold me while yet my tongue
Could scarcely cry "'weep! 'weep! 'weep! 'weep!"
So your chimneys I sweep & in soot I sleep.

There's little Tom Dacre, who cried when his head
That curled like a lamb's back, was shaved, so I said,
"Hush, Tom! never mind it, for when your head's bare,
You know that the soot cannot spoil your white hair."

And so he was quiet, & that very night,
As Tom was a-sleeping he had such a sight!
That thousands of sweepers, Dick, Joe, Ned, & Jack,
Were all of them locked up in coffins of black;

And by came an Angel who had a bright key,
And he opened the coffins & set them all free;
Then down a green plain, leaping, laughing they run,
And wash in a river and shine in the Sun.

Then naked & white, all their bags left behind,
They rise upon clouds, and sport in the wind.
And the Angel told Tom, if he'd be a good boy,
He'd have God for his father & never want joy.

And so Tom awoke; and we rose in the dark
And got with our bags & our brushes to work.
Though the morning was cold, Tom was happy & warm;
So if all do their duty, they need not fear harm.

Careful planning is important for all essays. You will initially have a lot of information about the text you are discussing, so it is important to think about what you should and shouldn't include.

Activity 3

Having read the poem at least twice, complete the questions below to help you develop your appreciation of what the poem is about and how Blake uses **poetic devices** to communicate these ideas.

a Who are the main characters in the poem?

b What is the poem about?

Activity 4

Complete the table below to help you **analyse** the poem.

Identify four poetic techniques Blake has used to communicate his ideas about childhood innocence.	Find an example of each poetic technique in the poem.	Explain what these poetic techniques convey about childhood innocence.
Symbolism	"Hush, Tom! never mind it, for when your head's bare, / You know that the soot cannot spoil your white hair."	The colour white is symbolic of Tom's initial childish innocence regarding the danger and difficulty of life as a chimney sweeper. Furthermore, the fact that his hair is being shaved symbolises the loss of Tom's innocence.
Onomatopoeia	**a**	**b**
Simile	**c**	**d**
Imagery	**e**	**f**

It's now time to plan the **thesis** for your essay. Your thesis will be your **argument** in response to the essay question with a series of smaller **thesis points** that further expand your argument. For this essay you will have three thesis points.

For example:

'The Second Coming' by William Butler Yeats is a modernist poem because it lacks a coherent structure, makes use of ambiguous symbolism and expresses a concern for the future of mankind.

In this example the thesis is in **bold** and the thesis points are underlined.

Your thesis for the essay in this unit will be:

William Blake's poem 'The Chimney Sweeper' communicates ideas about childhood innocence.

Activity 5

This question will help you plan your **thesis points**. What are three things about childhood innocence that Blake reveals to us in his poem? Use the words given below to help you write your answers.

For example: Childhood innocence is difficult to maintain in a corrupt world.

a hope ______________________________

b vulnerability ______________________________

c death ______________________________

Structure

A **critical analysis essay** adheres to the traditional structure of an essay. It features an **introductory** paragraph, **body** paragraphs and a **concluding** paragraph.

Introductory paragraph

An **introduction** can make or break the whole essay! It gives the reader their **first impression** of the essay's content. The introductory paragraph **outlines the text** you will be discussing and your argument—or **thesis**—in response to the essay question.

An effective introduction should:

- **get the reader engaged** and **interested** in the text and your argument
- **show that you understand** the question—this is best done by restating the essay question in your own words
- **briefly state your main thesis** and what text(s) will be discussed. As described above a thesis is essentially your argument in response to the question and typically includes around three supporting thesis points. Each of these points will be elaborated upon in at least one body paragraph.

Below is a sample introduction to the essay question 'How does Wordsworth use poetic devices in his poem "I Wandered Lonely as a Cloud" to show the reader how he feels about nature?'

> Poetry expresses an individual's most intense emotions in the least number of words. In the beautiful poem 'I Wandered Lonely as a Cloud' (1804) William Wordsworth uses a combination of rhyme, imagery, personification and tone to express his love for nature. The poem presents the reader with the beauty of nature, its freedom and the happiness nature brings to people.

This is a very basic introduction to show you the formula. In your own essay you may wish to add more information about the topic of your essay—this might be the text, the composer, the concept or the context that is central to the essay question.

Activity 1

Read the sample **introduction** above and then complete the following tasks.

a Underline the '**engaging opening**'.

b Highlight the title of the **text being discussed** in the body of the essay.

c Put a circle around the three main **thesis points** to be addressed in the essay. (Hint: these are listed in the last sentence of the introduction.)

Activity 2

It is now time for you to write the **introduction** to your essay on Blake's poem. Make sure that you look back through your planning to help identify your three main **thesis points**—these will be three things Blake is telling us about childhood innocence in the poem. Use your own paper.

Body paragraphs

The **body** of a **critical analysis essay** is made up of a number of linking paragraphs which provide **evidence** for the thesis points outlined in the introduction.

A paragraph is a group of about three or more sentences that express and develop one main idea. A **good paragraph** has the following elements:

* a **transition phrase** or clause that links each new paragraph to the previous one (e.g. Although the text deals with ... it also deals with ...)
* a **sentence that states** the main idea that is to be addressed
* a series of **explanatory sentences** which expand on the issue, provide evidence for ideas and answer the essay question
* **appropriate language**, which in this essay includes 'doing' verbs to explain the effects each technique has on the responder (e.g. illustrates, reveals, highlights)
* **connectives** to explain the relationships between key ideas and the essay question (e.g. therefore, so, since).

Clarity is a prime concern in effective essay writing so it is important to maintain a clear paragraph structure. This is especially important when writing a critical analysis essay.

The following is a suggested structure for each **body paragraph** of a critical analysis essay. It takes the form of a mnemonic—STEEL—which should help you remember all of the important parts of a really great body paragraph!

For each thesis point that you want to address you will need a new paragraph. This helps the reader to follow and understand your argument. The STEEL method will help you check if your paragraph (and analysis) is succinct. If you have each one of the elements you'll have a perfect paragraph.

Statement: The paragraph should start off with a statement that includes the thesis point and text you wish to address. A really strong statement will often begin with an abstract noun or noun phrase.

For example: 'The beauty of nature is shown ...' rather than
'The writer shows the beauty of nature ...'

Technique: Identify a technique that is used by the composer of the text to explore or reveal your thesis point.

Example: Support your thesis with an example of the technique used in the text. This may be a quote or brief outline of a scene from the text.

Effect: Explain the effect of this technique and why it is useful in exploring or revealing your thesis point and helping you answer the essay question.

Link: Link your evidence to your argument and to the importance of the ideas for a wider audience. Link back to the essay question.

Activity 3

The paragraph below uses all of the STEEL elements required for a great paragraph.

Wordsworth conveys the beauty of nature in his poem 'I Wandered Lonely as a Cloud'. He uses personification in the lines, 'Beside the lake, beneath the trees, / Fluttering and dancing in the breeze'. This poetic device creates an image of the beautiful daffodils, dancing as if they were human. Furthermore, this technique encourages the reader to imagine the small flowers moving in the wind and therefore appreciate the joy that Wordsworth feels because of the beauty of nature.

- **a** Label parts of the text with the letters of STEEL that they represent.
- **b** Circle the abstract noun used in the **statement**.
- **c** Circle the **doing verbs**.
- **d** Underline the **connective**.

Activity 4

Using the notes you made in the planning stage, especially those in the analysis table, write the first draft of your three **body paragraphs**. Remember: use the STEEL elements to help structure your paragraphs. Use your own paper for this task.

Concluding paragraph

The **concluding paragraph** of a critical analysis essay briefly returns to the essay question, sums up what has been discussed in the essay and makes a memorable comment on the topic. This paragraph must:

- **restate** the question in your own words
- **mention** the text or texts that have been discussed
- **sum up** the key points of your thesis.

Activity 5

In the following example of a good **concluding paragraph**, complete the following tasks:

- **a** underline words from the **essay question** (you can find this on page 49)
- **b** highlight the **name of the text and the composer**
- **c** number the **thesis points** from 1 to 3.

To conclude, William Wordsworth's poem 'I Wandered Lonely as a Cloud' is a beautiful example of the power of poetry to express intense feelings through an economical use of words. Wordsworth's clever use of poetic devices reveals his feelings that the beauty and freedom of nature have the ability to bring happiness to people.

Activity 6

It's now your turn to write the first draft of your concluding paragraph. Use your own paper. Good luck!

Language feature

Nominalisation

Nominalisation is to **change verbs or adjectives into nouns**. Nominalisation is an important language device because it allows you to present actions (verbs) as concepts or techniques (nouns) that are central to the argument you are making in your essay.

For example:
Wordsworth **personifies** the daffodils in his poem to show them as lively and beautiful.

↓

Personification of the daffodils shows them as lively and beautiful in Wordsworth's poem.

You will discover that using nominalisation in critical analysis essays is essential as it brings the focus of your reader to the **central concepts and techniques** being discussed. Concepts and techniques always take the form of abstract nouns.

For example:

metaphor	alienation	discovery
affection	sibilance	innocence
imagery	rejection	idealism

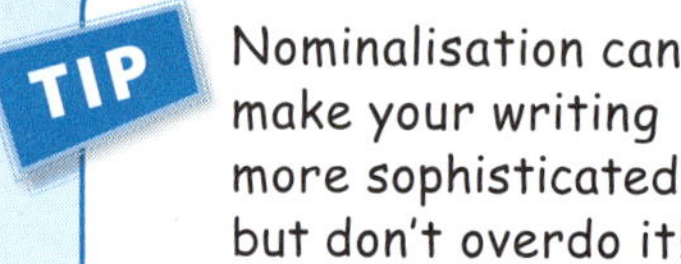

Nominalisation can make your writing more sophisticated, but don't overdo it!

Activity 1

Underline the **abstract conceptual noun** or nouns in each sentence below. The first one has been done for you.

- **a** The abandonment of the children was criticised by Hemingway.
- **b** The poem presents an image of elation.
- **c** Determination conquers apathy, always.
- **d** Shakespeare challenges the establishment of patriarchal expectations.
- **e** Cynicism regarding the treatment of mental patients was addressed by Foucault.
- **f** Confronting images of illness are evident in the novel.

Activity 2

Turn the following verbs and adverbs into **nouns** by adding the correct **suffix** from the list below.

Note: you may have to change the endings of the base words.

tion *ment* *ion* *ism* *ness* *ation*

a anticipate ____________ **b** operate ____________

c judge ____________ **d** amuse ____________

e hideous ____________ **f** holy ____________

g connote ____________ **h** criticise ____________

Activity 3

In the sentences below change the underlined central verb or adjective into a **noun**. You will need to restructure the sentences. The first one has been done for you.

a An excellent doctor is going to operate on my son.

My son's operation will be performed by an excellent doctor.

b What time will we depart?

c The way Mary reacted made me laugh.

d I am impressed by how long Eliot's poem is.

e Ms MacRae could see how eager the students were.

f The general feared that the enemy would invade soon.

Possessive apostrophe

The position of an **apostrophe** in relation to a noun provides information to readers about **ownership**. The correct use of a possessive apostrophe can be the cause of much confusion for young writers. However, once you know the following simple rules for success you will master the use of the possessive apostrophe in no time!

1. If the possessive noun is **singular**, always add *'s*.
   For example: dog → dog's   lady → lady's
2. If the possessive noun is **plural but does not end in *s***, always add 's.
   For example: children → children's   media → media's
3. If the possessive noun is **plural and ends in *s***, just add an apostrophe to the end.
   For example: fathers → fathers'   books → books'
4. If the possessive is **a name ending in *s*** add *'s*.
   For example: Keats → Keats's
5. Do **not** use an apostrophe when a noun is **plural rather than possessive**.
   For example: I ate three tomatoes for lunch.
   (No apostrophe is needed—*tomatoes* is a plural noun.)
   The tomato's skin is bruised. (An apostrophe is needed to show possession.)
6. Do **not** add an apostrophe to **verbs**.
   For example: He runs. (correct)
   He runs'. (incorrect)
   He run's. (incorrect)
7. Do **not** add an apostrophe to the **possessive form of *its***. (The dog wagged its tail.)

Activity 1

Circle the words spelt incorrectly in the sentences below. Write the correct spelling on the line provided.

a The poem illustrate's the beauty of Yeats's personal style. ______

b Imagery of night compels reader's to consider the sinister actions of the speaker.
______

c Within the pages of the novel are story's of childhood suffering. ______

d The final scene of the play presents Shakespeares most effective use of humour.
______

e Plaths narrative is confronting in its representation of mental illness. ______

f The joy of nature is captured beautifully through Wordsworths highly evocative images.
______

g I was impressed by the childrens response to the play. ______

h My favourite characters in *The Lord of the Rings* are the elf's. ______

Activity 2

Select the correct word in each of the sentences below.

a The turnout for the two (authors'/author's) combined workshop was sensational.

b Renaissance (painters'/painters) artworks continue to impress audiences today.

c The (illustrators/illustrator's) work is so intricate that it requires a magnifying glass to fully appreciate it.

d Tim Burton is one of the most original and inventive (filmmakers/filmmaker's).

e The (poet's/poets) of the Romantic movement celebrated individualism.

f My favourite (playwright's/playwrights) are Oscar Wilde and William Shakespeare.

Activity 3

Look at the pairs of nouns in brackets below. Make up sentences using each pair of nouns where the first is used as a **possessive noun**. The first one has been done for you.

a (scientist/discovery)
It was revealed that the scientist's celebrated discovery was in fact a fraud.

b (girls/bags)
______

c (computers/memories)
______

d (children/happiness)
______

e (poem/imagery)
______

You be the teacher

Below is a **body paragraph** for a critical analysis essay written by a Year 9 student. There are some errors in the structure of the paragraph, the use of the **apostrophe** and the spelling of some **nominalisations**. Can you correct the mistakes? Rewrite the paragraph with the **correct structure** and with the **correct spelling of all words**. Remember that the paragraph will follow the STEEL format.

Furthermore, the sibilance of the line, 'So your chimney's I sweep and in soot I sleep' creates a sombre tone, making the reader feel complicit in the childs abuse. Blakes use of confronting imagry, 'my father sold me while yet my tongue could scarcely cry "weep! weep! weep! weep!"' reminds the reader of the very young age at which the children were exploited. The innosense of children can lead to them being exploited by others'. Blake effectively uses' visual and aural image's to communicate the idea that childhood innocence is abused by dishonest people.

Now you write

It is now time for you to complete your own **critical analysis essay** on the poem by William Blake.

1. Before you write, take some time to look at the student writing sample on the following page as a guide to writing standards.

2. Once you have read the student writing sample, take some time to think about what you believe are the most important features of a critical analysis essay that you need to master. Use the lines below to jot down your answer to this question:
What do you find most difficult when writing this kind of text?

3. Now look at the informative text marking criteria on page vii to double-check that you understand the requirements for a really good piece of informative writing.
Remember that you have already done your planning and drafted your introductory paragraph, body paragraphs and concluding paragraph. Use your own paper. Good luck!

Looking at other students' writing

Write a critical analysis essay addressing the question below:
How does William Wordsworth convey ideas about nature in his poem 'I Wandered Lonely as a Cloud'?

Introduction
The introduction immediately engages with the ideas of the essay question. It names the poem and poet, as well as outlining the thesis and thesis points to be made in the essay.

Informative techniques
The student uses clear and precise language. Third-person narrative is used to create an objective, factual tone.

Text structure
The student uses the correct structure for a critical analysis essay, including introduction, body paragraphs and conclusion.

Paragraphing
Each paragraph features a thesis point statement, literary analysis, examples from the text to support ideas and a sentence linking back to the essay question.

ADVANCED SAMPLE

HOW DOES WILLIAM WORDSWORTH CONVEY IDEAS ABOUT NATURE IN HIS POEM 'I WANDERED LONELY AS A CLOUD'?

Poetry expresses an individual's most intense emotions in the least number of words. In the beautiful poem 'I Wandered Lonely as a Cloud' (1804) William Wordsworth uses a combination of rhyme, imagery, personification and tone to express his love for nature. The poem presents the reader with the beauty of nature, its freedom and the happiness nature brings to people.

William Wordsworth effectively creates a portrait of nature's beauty in his poem 'I Wandered Lonely as a Cloud'. Personification creates an image of the beautiful daffodils, 'Beside the lake, beneath the trees, / Fluttering and dancing in the breeze' where the daffodils are personified as 'dancing'. This technique encourages the reader to imagine the small flowers moving in the wind and therefore appreciate the joy that Wordsworth feels because of the beauty of nature.

Whilst the poem presents the beauty of nature it also expresses its freedom. Hyperbole effectively highlights the freedom of the daffodils by the water. The number of flowers is exaggerated in the image 'They stretched in never-ending line / Along the margin of a bay' to accentuate the liberty of the flowers as they bloom freely and seem to create a border between land and water. Wordsworth feels that nature is unrestrained and he admires and perhaps even envies its freedom.

In addition to communicating his feelings about the beauty and freedom of nature in the poem, Wordsworth also conveys his belief that nature brings happiness to people. Through the use of metaphor in the last stanza of the poem the poet claims that the flowers have the power to make him happy. He creates an image of happiness in the metaphor 'And then my heart with pleasure fills, / And dances with the daffodils'. This joyous image prompts the reader to feel moved by the happy flowers, just like Wordsworth, and thus further appreciate the natural world.

To conclude, William Wordsworth's poem 'I Wandered Lonely as a Cloud' is a beautiful example of the power of poetry to express intense feelings through an economical use of words. Through the clever use of language features specific to poetry Wordsworth reveals his feelings that the beauty and freedom of nature have the ability to bring happiness to people.

Vocabulary
Language choices are appropriate for the student's purpose. Complex vocabulary is used, including poetic terms such as personification, hyperbole and imagery.

Sentence structure
The student uses a combination of compound and complex sentences.

Ideas
Strong, detailed and well-explained ideas that are relevant to the topic are included in each body paragraph.

Cohesion
Each paragraph opens with a succinct thesis point statement. All paragraphs focus on the central topic of the essay: the poem 'I Wandered Lonely as a Cloud'.

Punctuation
Complex punctuation is used correctly.

Spelling
All words are spelt correctly, including technical and complex words.

UNIT SIX

Informative texts
Radio interview transcripts

Understanding the question

Script a radio interview about youth homelessness.

Type of question

This question is asking you to write a particular type of informative text—a **radio interview transcript**. A radio interview is an exchange between a journalist or presenter and an invited guest about a specific topic or issue.

A radio interview transcript is structured in a similar way to a drama script, as it is essentially a **conversation between two or more people**. For this task you are required to write both sides of the interview. You are being asked to write a radio interview transcript about youth homelessness.

Features of a radio interview

- Aims to inform people about current issues
- Presents a range of perspectives on an issue
- Typically is between two people, one interviewing and one being interviewed
- Questions and answers may use evidence such as facts and statistics
- Features objective and subjective language

Read closely the question that you need to write for this chapter and answer the following questions.

1 What does the verb **script** mean?

2 What are three differences between a **transcript** and a **written report**?

3 What are the two **content words** in this question and what do they mean when combined?

Planning and organisation

Typically a radio interview features two types of people: the host of the segment or show who asks questions, and the invited guest who answers the questions. For this task, you will adopt both roles. This requires a lot of careful planning as well as research.

Careful planning and organisation is important when writing a radio interview transcript. Make sure you spend enough time gathering your information and planning before you put pen to paper.

Activity 1

The first step when writing a transcript for a radio interview is to decide **who you will interview**. In the space below, list six types of people who would be suitable as an **interviewee** to provide information about the topic of youth homelessness.

Activity 2

The next step is to come up with your **interview questions**. Use the star-bursting technique. On the star below are six points. Each point is labelled with a question starter. Try to devise two or three questions about your topic using each question starter. It's a good idea to think about what types of responses you want from your interviewee and structure your questions to get these responses. An example has been done for you.

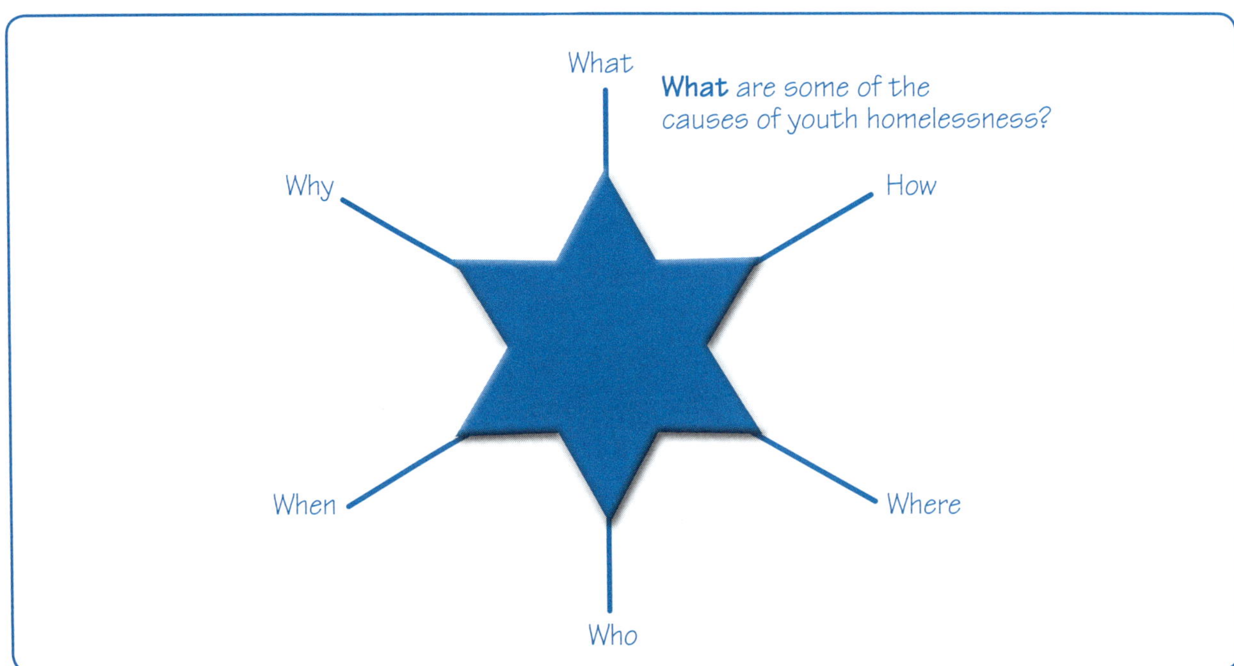

Activity 3

Select four questions from the task above that you will use for your **radio interview**. Write them below. Don't forget to consider the **audience** and **purpose** of your radio interview, as this may influence the type of questions you ask.

a ____________________

b ____________________

c ____________________

d ____________________

Activity 4

For this chapter's writing task, you must adopt the role of the interviewer and the interviewee. In order to answer the questions that you have written, you will probably need to do some research on the topic of youth homelessness. Record your findings in the box below.

Here are some useful websites full of information about this issue.
Salvation Army's Oasis: **http://salvos.org.au/oasis/**
Youth Off The Streets: **http://www.youthoffthestreets.com.au/**
Kids Under Cover: **http://www.kuc.org.au/**

Structure

The type of interview that you are writing is an **explanation interview**. It involves the interviewer asking the interviewee questions about a specific topic they have expertise in, specifically with the purpose of informing listeners.

Most radio interviews stick to a specific structure: an **opening monologue** followed by a series of **questions**, ending with a **closing monologue**.

Opening monologue

The **opening monologue** of a radio interview has three functions:

- to **welcome** listeners
- to provide a quick **overview** of the topic
- to **introduce** the invited guest experts.

Activity 1

Below is the **opening monologue** for a radio interview about domestic cats. Unfortunately the sentences are out of order. Number the sentences in the correct order from 1 to 3.

______ This morning we will be talking about domestic cats and answering the questions: how do I train my cat to use the litter box, to use the scratching pole and to only eat two meals per day?

______ Good morning listeners and welcome to *The Morning Report* with your host, Joseph Jones.

______ First, I'd like to welcome our guest expert, Professor Judy Nguyen, who is an academic at Sydney University, specialising in animal behaviour.

Activity 2

It's time for you to draft the **opening monologue** for your radio interview about youth homelessness. Use your own paper for this activity.

Body

The **body** of a radio interview consists of a **series of questions and answers**. It is a good idea to begin this section by ordering your questions in a logical sequence.

Activity 3

Look at the four **questions** below written by a student for a radio interview about smoking. Put them in the order they should be asked by numbering them from 1 to 4.

_____ How can people quit smoking? _____ What prompts people to start smoking?

_____ What is the cost of smoking? _____ What does smoking do to the human body?

Activity 4

Go back to your planning notes and write your four **questions** below, in the order they should be asked.

1 ____________________

2 ____________________

3 ____________________

4 ____________________

The next step is writing the **answers** to the questions. For this radio interview you will be interviewing only one person: the guest expert. Think carefully about the types of **language** your expert would use. You can check out the suggested language features to include in a radio interview on page 61.

Activity 5

It's now time to write the expert's **answers** to one of the questions you asked, based on the internet research you did previously. Use your notes from the planning stage to help you. An example has been given below.

Interviewer: What are the benefits of a good night's sleep?
Interviewee: There are many benefits to having a quality night's sleep. Research suggests that sleeping at least 8 hours per night can improve your memory, reduce stress levels and contribute to heart health. It is important that sleep is unbroken. Yes, this can be hard with our busy lives, but it can be achieved by removing digital devices like mobile phones from the bedroom.

Closing monologue

The **closing monologue** of a radio interview must do four things:

- **thank the expert** for sharing their expertise
- **summarise the main points** about the topic that were discussed
- **thank the listeners** for tuning in to your radio show/segment
- **remind the listeners to tune in next time**, telling them the topic and the time the show is on.

Using your own paper, draft the **closing monologue** for your radio interview about youth homelessness.

Language feature

Tone

Tone in writing reflects the **perspective, attitude or mood** of a character or writer. Using tone in your informative or persuasive writing helps your reader understand what your feelings are towards a particular topic, which can ultimately influence how the reader feels about the topic.

The tone used by a speaker in a radio interview can change many times. The tone of the interviewer may be serious and formal when asking questions, but when welcoming the listeners it may be playful and casual.

Tone is conveyed in many ways including:

- **Personal language**. When a speaker or writer is sharing their personal experiences related to an issue or topic, they will likely use **first-person narrative** (e.g. *mine, our, we, I*), and colloquial language (e.g. *She'll be right, No problem*).
- **Impersonal language**. When a speaker or writer is discussing an issue that is very **serious** and which affects a large number of people, they will probably use **third-person narrative** (e.g. *they, them, their*) and formal language (e.g. *The number of casualties is predicted to rise in the next two days*).
- **Objective language**. This refers to the use of **statistics** and other **data** to support ideas. Objective language is similar to impersonal language, in that it often uses third-person narrative.

  For example: The National Department of Transportation estimates drowsy driving to be responsible for 1550 fatalities and 40,000 nonfatal injuries annually in the United States.
- **Subjective language**. This is language that reveals **personal opinion and bias**. It typically uses **first-** and **second-person narrative** (e.g. *me, my, our, your*).

  For example: My belief is that it isn't possible to get a good night's sleep. Life is just too stressful.
- **Emotive language**. This is language that clearly communicates a person's **strong attitude** towards a topic.

  For example: When someone is not supportive of a decision they may say they are *disgusted, incensed* or *embarrassed.*

The **topic of the interview will usually determine the tone**. If the content of an interview is very serious, such as cancer, homelessness or crime, it is likely that the tone will be formal and serious, and the language mostly impersonal and objective. Similarly, if the content of the interview is more light-hearted, such as favourite films, holiday destinations or food, the tone is likely to be more upbeat and relaxed, and the language more personal and subjective and even emotive.

Also, with spoken texts such as radio interviews, **aspects of delivery** such as pace, pause and pitch can affect the tone.

Types of tones you may find in writing: grave, amused, respectful, casual, sarcastic, authoritative, joyful, anxious, serious, humorous, sad, threatening.

Activity 1

Below is an interview question with three different responses. For each response choose the **tone** from the box below which best describes it. Then underline the **language features** which help to convey this tone.

emotive	factual	light-hearted

Interview question: What are the negatives associated with keeping a cat?

Well, I can't speak for others, but my cat Charlie, he wakes me up at 4 am every morning [laughs]. He scratches at my door because he wants to be fed. I guess if that's as bad as it gets, cats are pretty good pets.

a Tone: ______________________________

There is a range of negatives associated with cat ownership. These negatives include unwanted pregnancy, health problems such as heartworm and feline cancer, not to mention the inevitable pain associated with the loss of a pet when they succumb to a paralysis tick. The average domestic cat costs over $1000 a year to keep, so for many families the biggest negative associated with cat ownership is cost.

b Tone: ______________________________

Cats could quite literally bring about the complete extinction of a number of small birds and mammal species. Irresponsible pet owners fail to desex their cats, resulting in unwanted litters which invariably are dumped in nature reserves and state parks. These feral cats are horribly disruptive to our already vulnerable native species.

c Tone: ______________________________

Activity 2

Read the sentences below about playing video games. Choose the **tone** from the box that matches each sentence.

sad	sarcastic	anxious	casual	authoritative	confident

a Yeah, I don't mind games. They're pretty cool. ______________________________

b My son plays games all the time. All night long, for hours and hours at a time. It can't be healthy, can it? What if he can't cope with reality? ______________________________

c Video games kill thousands of people every year. Oh, wait. No, they don't.

____

d Children under the age of 12 should not play video games. ______________________________

e It's been a long hard road since we lost our Jessie to lung cancer. ______________________________

f Being a professor of 17th century literature, I feel my interpretation of Shakespeare's sonnet is entirely credible. ______________________________

Activity 3

Each question gives you a topic and two tones. Write two sentences for each topic, one in each tone. The first question has been done for you.

a Topic: Junk food
Tone: serious/light-hearted

serious: According to a recent study, sleeplessness is a cause of people eating more junk food.

light-hearted: I just adore eating chocolate and ice cream topped with chocolate buttons—yummy!

b Topic: Life after high school
Tone: anxious/light-hearted

---

c Topic: Dogs in public places
Tone: amused/annoyed

---

d Topic: Working out at the gym

Tone: casual/serious

Spotlight on spelling

Compound plurals

A **compound noun** is a noun that consists of two or more words. Most compound nouns are created by adding two nouns together such as *football, toothpaste* or *fish tank*.

There are **three different types** of compound nouns. Each type of compound noun has its own rules for making the plural.

Open: This is when a compound noun is made of more than one word, usually two or three words separated by spaces.

For example: doctor of philosophy, trade unions

Plural rule: Add *s* or *es* to the base word. The base word is the most significant noun.
For example: in the compound noun *doctor of philosophy*, the most significant noun is *doctor*.
This is the word that becomes plural by adding *s*.
doctor of philosophy → doctor**s** of philosophy

In the compound noun *trade union* the most significant noun is *union* so that is the noun that is made plural.
trade union → trade union**s**

Hyphenated: This is when a compound noun is made by joining two or more words with a hyphen.

For example: mother-in-law, right-of-way

Plural rule: Add *s* or *es* to the base word. The base word is the most significant noun.

For example: in the compound noun *mother-in-law*, the most significant noun is *mother*. This is the word that becomes plural by adding *s*. Similarly, in *right-of-way* the most significant noun is *right*. This is the word that becomes plural by adding *s*.
mother-in-law → mother**s**-in-law

Closed: This is when a compound noun is created by adding two words together to create one word.

For example: headband, breakfast

Plural rule: When the compound noun is only one word, you simply add *s* or *es* to create the plural form.
database → database**s**

Activity 1

Match the words to make **compound nouns**. The first has been done for you.

a	sauce	house
b	out	looker
c	soft	shine
d	check	turn
e	sun	ware
f	hard	pan
g	green	put
h	up	out
i	on	ware

Activity 2

Write the compound nouns below as plurals.

a takeoff ______________________

b attorney-general ______________________

c brother-in-law ______________________

d sergeant major ______________________

e passer-by ______________________

f hanger-on ______________________

g handful ______________________

h mouthful ______________________

You be the teacher

Below is a **body paragraph** for a radio interview transcript written by a Year 9 student. There are some errors in the structure of the paragraph and the spelling of some words. Can you correct the mistakes? Rewrite the paragraph with the **correct structure** and with the **correct spelling of all words**.

Interviewer: What are some causes of youth homelessness?
Interviewee: Other known reasons why young people find themselves homeless are mental illness, drug or alcohol abuse or lack of affordable houseing. The primary factor is a lack of stabillity in the family home. There are many reasons why young people become homless. There are a vareity of reasons why home life may be unstable, including domestic violence, poverty and family breakdown.

Now you write

It is now time for you to write the **script for a radio interview** about youth homelessness.

1 Before you write, take some time to look at the student writing sample on the following page as a guide to writing standards.

2 Once you have read the student writing sample, take some time to think about what you believe are the most important features of a radio interview transcript that you need to master. Use the lines below to jot down your answer to this question:
What do you find most difficult when writing this kind of text?

3 Now look at the informative text marking criteria on page vii to double-check that you understand the requirements for a really good piece of informative writing.

Remember that you have already done your planning and drafted your opening monologue, your interview questions and your closing monologue. Use your own paper. Good luck!

Looking at other students' writing

Radio interview transcripts:
Script a radio interview about smoking.

Introduction
The introduction alerts the audience to the purpose of the interview: to inform listeners about the causes and effects of smoking. The opening sentence welcomes listeners.

Informative language
The student uses clear and precise language. Formal, objective, impersonal language is used by the interviewee to explain and inform. Some informal, personal language is used by the interviewer to create a connection with the audience.

Text structure
The student uses the correct structure for a radio interview: opening monologue, series of questions and answers, and concluding monologue.

Paragraphing
Each paragraph focuses on information about one specific question.

ADVANCED SAMPLE

SCRIPT A RADIO INTERVIEW ABOUT SMOKING.

Interviewer: Good afternoon, you're on KRD2204, with me, Gary Johnston, host of *The Johnston Report*. Today we're going to be talking about smoking—why do people do it, the impact it has on health and how we can help you quit.

Interviewer: Firstly, I'd like to welcome our guest expert, Dr Janet Hoskings, from the Department of Health, who will be here to answer the big questions about smoking cigarettes. Thanks so much for joining us today Janet. I'd like to start with the obvious question: what is it that prompts people to start smoking?

Interviewee: Thanks so much for having me, Gary. Well, that is an obvious question but unfortunately there is no simple or obvious answer. Some of the most common reasons why people begin smoking include having parents or family members who smoke, being exposed through films or television to images of celebrities who smoke, and using smoking as a stress reliever.

Interviewer: So it's a complicated thing. You mentioned in there, seeing celebrities smoke. Is this why we now have a ban on having people smoking on television?

Interviewee: Absolutely. Research shows that people are highly influenced by what they see in the media, especially on television, and through the hard work of the department and other organisations, we've been successful in having smoking banned from television.

Interviewer: So that brings me to my next question. Why is it so bad to smoke?

Interviewee: Well, there are so many negative consequences of smoking. Obviously I can't list them all here today, but the main one is the significantly increased risk of developing lung cancer as well as cancer of the tongue and lips. Smoking causes nine out of 10 lung cancers in Australia. There are also less well-known consequences including increased rates of impotency in men and increased rates of macular degeneration in both genders.

Interviewer: It surprises me that with such shocking statistics around smoking that people continue to smoke. I suppose it's because it's so addictive. What can people do to try and quit smoking?

Interviewee: Well Australians are very fortunate because there are a number of support groups available to people who want to quit smoking. The Australian Government continues to fund Quitline, which is a free service that allows anyone to ring up and get advice and support over the phone from trained health-care providers.

Interviewer: Well that is a fantastic service. Thank you so much for joining us today, Dr Hoskings. For those of you at home who are interested in Quitline, the number is 137848. We're going to take a small break. We'll be back after these messages from our sponsors.

Vocabulary
Language is appropriate. Complex vocabulary is used and appropriate to an informative radio interview, e.g. *consequences*, *measures*.

Sentence structure
The student uses a variety of simple, compound and complex sentences.

Ideas
Questions are clear. Ideas that are relevant to the topic are included in each interviewee answer. Ideas are detailed and well explained.

Cohesion
Each paragraph opens with a succinct and focused answer to the question. All paragraphs focus on the central idea of the topic: the causes and effects of smoking.

Punctuation
Complex punctuation is used correctly.

Spelling
All words are spelt correctly, including technical and complex words.

UNIT SEVEN

Informative texts
Magazine articles

Understanding the question

Research issues relating to teenagers' use of technology.
Write a magazine article documenting your findings.

Type of question

This question is asking you to write a particular type of informative text—a **magazine article**.

The word **research** informs you of the need to find out more about the topic: young people and technology.

The question uses the word **issues** which suggests that there are problems associated with teenage use of technology, and this is what you will need to find out about.

Features of a magazine article

- Aims to inform readers about current events or topics
- Organises information under subheadings
- Structures information from most important or interesting to least important
- Uses language that is mostly factual and objective, but may use personal and informal language to increase engagement
- Typically uses third-person narrative to focus the reader on the information rather than on the writer but may use first person if article is about personal experiences

1 What does the word **research** mean?

____

2 The word **document** can be a verb or a noun. In this question, it is a verb. What does it mean?

____

3 List two topics that magazine articles could be written about for each of the given magazine titles below.

a *Men's Health*

______________ ______________

b *National Geographic*

______________ ______________

c *Practical Parenting*

______________ ______________

d *Gardening Australia*

______________ ______________

Planning and organisation

The first step before researching a topic for a magazine article is to **brainstorm**. This allows you to identify what you already know about a topic and also identify specific areas for **further research**.

Activity 1

On the spider maps below, add everything you know about each topic. One piece of information has been written on each map to help you get started.

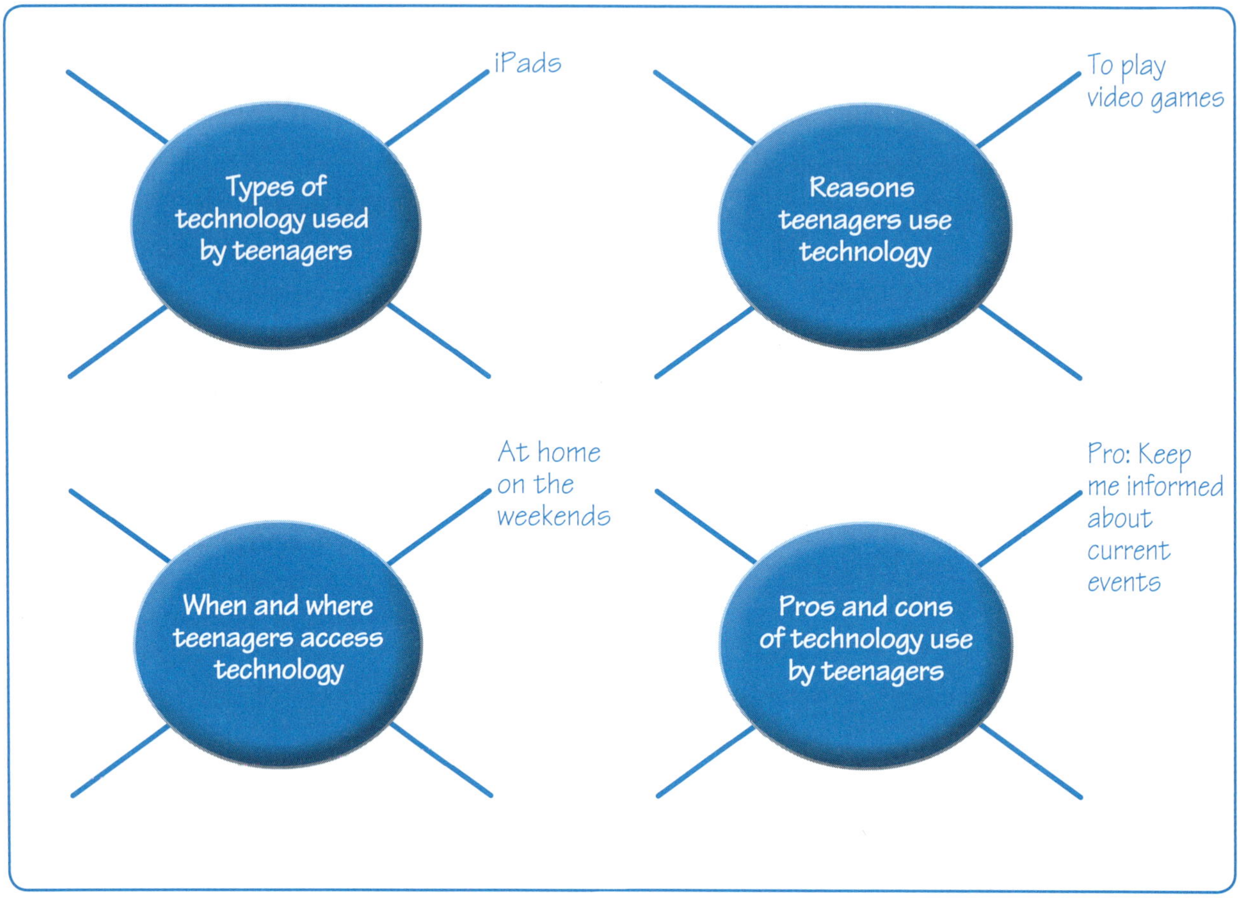

Types of technology used by teenagers
- iPads

Reasons teenagers use technology
- To play video games

When and where teenagers access technology
- At home on the weekends

Pros and cons of technology use by teenagers
- Pro: Keep me informed about current events

Activity 2

Use the internet to further develop your ideas about the four subheadings above.

Remember: when searching on the internet you should only use **key words**, not complete sentences or questions. For this topic you might use the following search terms:

- technology + teenagers
- negatives + teenagers + technology
- teenagers + technology + access.

Try to find factual information such as **statistics** to support each subheading. Select two or three points for each subheading. Decide on an order in which to discuss each point.

If you cannot access the internet, use your own experiences and knowledge about teenagers and technology to further develop your ideas. Write your research on your own paper.

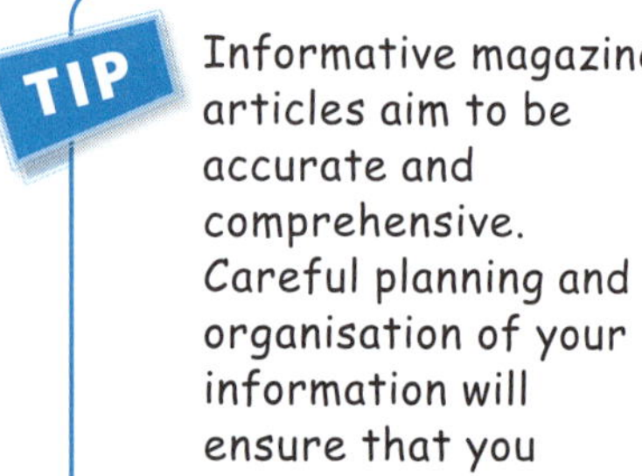

Structure

A **magazine article** follows a standard **structure**: **introductory paragraph**, **body paragraphs** and **concluding paragraph**. A magazine article always begins with a **headline** (e.g. *The Four-Hour Work Week*) and sometimes a subheading. The headline has two important functions:

* to grab the reader's attention
* to summarise the main focus of the article.

Activity 1

Match the headline to the magazine article topic.

a Powder Power!	**i** Healthy eating
b Making Affordable Art	**ii** Arts and crafts
c Be a Bully Buster	**iii** Bullying in schools
d Get Gorgeous	**iv** Beauty
e Hobby Crafts Career	**v** Child models
f Is it Healthy to be a Vegan?	**vi** Successful business
g Rise of the Catwalk Kids	**vii** Protein supplements

Introductory paragraph

The first, or **introductory**, paragraph of a magazine article has three purposes:

* to **establish the writer's tone**—whether it is serious, playful or emotive
* to **create a relationship** between the writer and the reader
* to **provide an introduction** to the topic, usually with background information.

Activity 2

Below are two **introductory paragraphs**. They have different styles—one is informal and personal and the other is formal and objective. Read them carefully and then, on the lines below, list the differences in the language and style of each (e.g. first-person narrative or use of statistics).

a Informal and personal introductory paragraph:

It's early on a Saturday morning and I'm busy stuffing lolly bags whilst my husband ties string around doughnuts. After hours of agonising, we decided on a train theme for Mr 7's birthday party. It seems children's birthday parties are the event on the social calendar these days. And don't we know that everyone will be watching?

b Formal and objective introductory paragraph:

Unattainable beauty ideals have contributed to the increasing rates of eating disorders amongst young men and women. The most significant influence in establishing these ideals is the media. Beauty and fashion magazines continue to push unattainable ideals relating to weight, the clarity of one's skin and the types of clothes and products individuals buy.

Activity 3

Write the **introductory paragraph** for your magazine article on technology and teenagers. Use your own paper for this activity.

Body paragraphs

The **body** of a **magazine article** is a series of paragraphs that elaborate further on the topic. The paragraphs provide **evidence** in the form of quotes from interviews, **references** to existing research or relevant **statistics**. Often the body paragraphs in a magazine article are arranged under **subheadings** to help the reader navigate the information in the article.

Activity 4

Below are five **subheadings**. Underline the two that would fit best with an article about the rising popularity of young-adult fiction.

Best-selling young-adult fiction authors

Boring books are left unread

First-time novelists intrigue young readers

Books become films

Video games more appealing than novels

Sometimes magazine articles feature **boxed text**, which is usually a **key quote** from the article that **summarises one aspect** of the magazine article. This boxed text is presented in a bigger font and positioned centrally within the body of the article. Its purpose is to encourage a person to read the article. There are three main types of information that are included in the boxed section:

- a startling **statistic**
- an **interviewee's comment**
- a sentence that summarises the **main points** of the article.

Activity 5

Match each sentence to the correct type of boxed text below.

a Startling statistic	**i** My dog is my best friend!
b Summary of main points in article	**ii** Depression is a black dog that chases me each night.
c Summary of main points in article	**iii** Three out of four internet users shop online.
d Interviewee comment	**iv** Literacy involves learning to speak, read, listen, write and understand.
e Interviewee comment	**v** The biggest mistake parents make is trying to be friends with their teenage children.

Activity 6

Go back to the spider map notes on page 68. Choose one of the four subheadings and write a **body paragraph** about that subheading.

Concluding paragraph

The purpose of a **concluding paragraph** is to **restate the main points** of the magazine article. If appropriate, the concluding paragraph may include a **call to action** or encourage a change of attitude or behaviour.

For example:
If you've been reading this article and thinking, 'Hey that's me!' then it's time to start getting healthy and fit. Call your local gym, go to the greengrocer, and start taking care of yourself. If you don't, who will?

Activity 7

Below are three draft **concluding paragraphs** written by a student for a magazine article about cybersafety. Select the one you think is best and briefly explain why you chose it.

Example one:
You should always be safe online. Don't ever share your passwords or your personal details. It is so easy to get hacked online. That's my final message for this article—be safe.

Example two:
Most people behave badly online. The sense that you are protected by the screen gives people the chance to interact with others in ways they would not normally. Simply read the comments section of any online news source and you will see what I mean.

Example three:
Ultimately, young people must develop the skills to protect their privacy online and to learn proper online etiquette. Schools are an essential factor in the development of the skills, whether through frequent supervised use of the internet, or through participation in cybersafety workshops. Our young people should feel safe online, and it is only education that can ensure this.

Activity 8

Write the **concluding paragraph** for your magazine article about teenagers and technology. Use your own paper for this task.

Language feature

Jargon

Jargon is the use by writers, in a particular occupation or field of activity, of **words and phrases** which have a **particular meaning to others in that field**. These terms are often so specialised that you may not understand what they mean if you are not a member of the field.

For example: Gaming jargon: FPS, developer, NPC
Social media jargon: LOL, like, Tweet, hashtag
Medical jargon: alpha blockers, ECG, agonal

The type of jargon that you will use in a magazine article will depend on the topic of your article. If it is about soccer, you will use jargon associated with that sport.

It is important to remember that you should not use jargon that your reader does not know without explaining it to them. If your reader does not understand the jargon they will lose interest, as they will not understand the content of the article. Strategies to overcome the inappropriate use of jargon include making sure you explain or give everyday meanings to jargon.

Activity 1

Match the **jargon** to the appropriate subject or occupation.

a military	**i** console game
b police	**ii** LOL
c gaming	**iii** casualties
d politics	**iv** left-wing
e texting	**v** the nine to five
f business	**vi** suspect

Activity 2

Match the **jargon** with the appropriate **magazine article** topic.

a follicles	**i** rock music
b amps	**ii** laptop computers
c blank verse	**iii** hair beauty
d RAM	**iv** school lunches
e nutrition	**v** Shakespeare's poetry

Language feature

Emotive language

Emotive language is the use of words to stir specific emotions in the reader. In magazine articles, emotive language is used to provoke a **specific response from the reader**, such as shock, sympathy or anger. Whilst many magazine articles are informative, they often also have **persuasive** elements. Emotive language can be a useful persuasive device.

For example:
Many believe that if children are not taught evolution, big bang and relativism, it could be disastrous.

In the above example, the word *disastrous* is the emotive word used to show the concern of the speaker relating to children's lack of scientific knowledge.

You need to be careful when using emotive language in magazine articles, as your main purpose is to inform, and an overuse of emotive language can make a writer seem biased and unbalanced. Use emotive language sparingly but effectively to present the impact of experiences and ideas on others.

Emotive language will often be used in quotes from sources, such as witnesses, experts or other interviewees.

For example:
The organiser of the Plymouth, Massachusetts, anti-Thanksgiving march stated that, 'We call it a National Day of Mourning because that day marks the end of our lives as we knew them—our land had been stolen.'

In the above examples the emotive word *stolen* reflects the anger felt by the interviewee. So too do the words *the end of our lives as we knew them.*

Activity 3

Circle all of the **emotive words** in the passage below. Then briefly explain whether the use of emotive language in this passage makes you believe or doubt the writer's point of view overall.

Last week was particularly heartbreaking. We rescued a tiny baby ring-tailed possum which had been ripped from the back of its mother by a feral cat. It had deep bloody claw marks in its back. I was crying as my husband bandaged it up. It was shocking to see the damage that the cat could do. This is why it is essential that feral cats are brought under control immediately.

____

____

Activity 4

Underline the **emotive words** in the sentences below and write an alternative objective word to replace each one. The first question has been done for you.

a The cat murdered the baby possum. killed

b The number of young people smoking is disgusting. ____________

c The politicians bullied the opposition into accepting their policy. ____________

d Children today are addicted to video games. ____________

e Allen was pestered by the media for his side of the story. ____________

f Dr Patterson is said to have agonised over the decision to amputate the boy's leg. ____________

Words with a silent *e*

If a word ends with a silent *e* (an *e* that is not pronounced) and the suffix begins with a vowel sound (*a*, *e*, *i*, *o* or *u*) drop the *e* before adding the suffix.

For example:
debate + *ing* → debat**ing**

However, you usually keep the *e* when adding a suffix that begins with a consonant.

For example:
base + *ment* → base**ment**

There are some exceptions. Words ending in *ce* and *ge* keep the *e* when adding the suffixes *able* and *ous*.

For example:
change + *able* → change**able**

Activity 1

Add the given suffix to each word below.

- **a** cane + ing ______________
- **b** dose +ed ______________
- **c** come + ing ______________
- **d** abase + ment ______________
- **e** mime + ing ______________
- **f** bite + ing ______________
- **g** pace + ed ______________
- **h** accurate + ly ______________
- **i** false + ly ______________
- **j** gentle + ly ______________
- **k** grave + ly ______________
- **l** lone + some ______________

Activity 2

Some of the sentences below contain incorrectly spelt words.

Write the **correct spelling** of any incorrect words on the line below. If all words are correctly spelt write **correct**.

- **a** Mr Anderson put forward his criticism of the building as positivly as possible. ______________
- **b** The group will continue to protest against caged eggs. ______________
- **c** There will be an ongoing investigation into the impact of minning on the local environment. ______________
- **d** He did not include correct citation of the works used. ______________
- **e** My children behave like dotting parents when they care for the orphaned bilbies. ______________
- **f** The company had hopped to come to a settlement earlier in the year. ______________
- **g** One sport that has become popular in the Lakehaven area is tubing. ______________
- **h** One will often see a young child totting a favourite teddy bear around the local shops. ______________
- **i** The bushfire came as a timly reminder that we must not take for granted the power of nature. ______________
- **j** The area is densely populated. ______________

You be the teacher

Below is a **body paragraph** for a magazine article written by a Year 10 student. There are some errors in the structure of the paragraph and the spelling of some words with a **silent *e***. Can you correct the mistakes? Rewrite the paragraph with the **correct structure** and with the **correct spelling of all words**.

This sustained use of technology may have a long-term impact on young people's health, something that researchers must begin to assess. Teenagers today have grown up indulgeing in daily access to a wide range of digital technologies. Once they are up and ready for the day, teenagers move on to school where they access technology, such as iPads and laptops, designed to positivly enhance their learning. Many young people wake up in the morning and check their phones hopfful to find text messages, Facebook comments, likes on Instagram and retweets on Twitter.

Now you write

It is now time for you to complete your own **magazine article** on teenagers' use of technology.

1. Before you write, take some time to look at the student writing sample on the following page as a guide to writing standards.

2. Once you have read the student writing sample, take some time to think about what you believe are the most important features of a magazine article that you need to master. Use the lines below to jot down your answer to this question: What do you find most difficult when writing this kind of text?

3. Now look at the informative text marking criteria on page vii to double-check that you understand the requirements for a really good piece of informative writing.

   Remember that you have already done your planning and drafted your introductory paragraph, one body paragraph and concluding paragraph. Use your own paper. Good luck!

Looking at other students' writing

Magazine articles:

Write a magazine article about body image.

Introduction
The introduction alerts the audience to the topic of the magazine article—body image.

Informative language
The student uses clear and precise language. Third-person narrative is used to create an objective, factual tone.

Text structure
The student uses the correct structure for a magazine article, including an introduction, a series of paragraphs introduced by subheadings, and a concluding paragraph. A boxed text section is also included.

Paragraphing
Each paragraph features detailed information about specific elements of the topic, relevant to subheadings used.

ADVANCED SAMPLE

WRITE A MAGAZINE ARTICLE ABOUT BODY IMAGE.
THE BODY—BEAUTY AND THE BEAST

Unattainable beauty ideals have contributed to the increasing rates of eating disorders amongst young men and women. The most significant influence in establishing these ideals is the media. Beauty and fashion magazines continue to push unattainable ideals relating to weight, the clarity of one's skin and the types of clothes and products individuals buy.

What is body image?

The term 'body image' is used frequently in the media, but what does it actually mean? Body image is essentially the way that an individual perceives their body, and how they assume others perceive them. Many people have a negative perception of what their body looks like, resulting in feelings of unhappiness and a desire to change their body.

> The media, family and friends can negatively or positively affect the image an individual has of their body.

Dying to be thin

Unfortunately having a negative body image can lead to quite serious conditions such as eating disorders like anorexia nervosa or bulimia, as well as depression and even self-harm. The number of young people suffering from eating disorders has doubled in the last 10 years, with over 90 per cent of all cases occurring in females. This is a troubling sign of the pressure to be thin that young girls feel.

Battling beauty myths

The influence of the media on negative body image cannot be underestimated. The use of very thin women in advertising and in film and television creates false ideals for young women in society. Furthermore the use of excessively muscular men has resulted in increased anxiety about body image in young men. A recent study of 600 schoolchildren revealed that they are increasingly feeling pressured by the relentless marketing aimed at them. Advertisements suggest that external beauty is more important than inner beauty, a dangerous notion.

Young people around the world continue to be confronted with unrealistic representations of beauty via media, social media and marketing. The only way for young people to combat this is to feel supported by friends and family and to learn that inner beauty is longer lasting than physical beauty. For this, we can all take responsibility.

Vocabulary
Language is appropriate. Complex vocabulary is used and appropriate for a magazine article, e.g. *unattainable, perception*.

Sentence structure
A variety of simple, compound and complex sentences are used.

Ideas
Strong ideas relevant to the topic are included in each body paragraph. Ideas are detailed, well explained and supported by research and statistics.

Cohesion
Each paragraph opens with a succinct topic sentence. All paragraphs focus on the central topic of the magazine article: body image.

Punctuation
Complex punctuation is used correctly.

Spelling
All words are spelt correctly, including technical and complex words.

UNIT EIGHT

8

Informative texts
Web pages

Understanding the question

Compose an informative web page about a controversial historical figure.

Type of question

You are required to write information for a **web page**. The word ***informative*** is the clue to what type of web page you should write. You are not being asked to present your personal opinion on the topic—you are being asked to provide information about the given topic for your readers.

You must develop a **structured response** that helps your reader better **understand the focus** of the question: a controversial historical figure.

Features of a web page

- Aims to provide information about a specific person, topic or event
- Structured in paragraphs
- Includes factual information and sometimes statistics and dates
- Has a heading and subheadings
- Includes images or video to support written text
- Includes hyperlinks to help readers discover further information about key aspects of the person, topic or event
- Uses objective and formal language

1 The key **content word** in the question for this unit is *controversial.*
Circle the three words from the list below that are **synonyms** for *controversial.*

divisive	unpopular
contentious	cruel
brilliant	provocative

2 Identify one controversial figure from each of the given areas.

Television: ______________________________

Music: ______________________________

Politics: ______________________________

TIP Web pages include hyperlinks to further information, so it is essential that you do some planning beforehand to find this information.

Planning and organisation

Research is essential when you are asked to compose a web page.

Activity 1

Write a list of three controversial historical figures, and complete the table below. You may need to use the internet or ask an adult to help complete this task.

Name	Brief description of individual	Reason(s) for being controversial

Activity 2

Select one of the above figures to base your web page on. It is now time to research this person. You may choose to research your topic online, read some non-fiction books from a library or ask someone who you feel has expertise on the topic. Using that information, complete the table below.

Name	
Date of birth/ Date of death	
Birthplace	
Significant life events	
Controversial events/experiences	
People's attitudes towards this person	

Structure

Informative **web pages** typically have a formal **structure**. This structure features three main parts:

- **introductory paragraph**
- series of **body paragraphs** that outline the most important information about the topic and which may also include hyperlinks to relevant sites
- **concluding paragraph** that provides links to further information about the topic.

Introductory paragraph

The **introductory paragraph** provides a general **outline** of the topic.

For example:
One of the most popular styles of music in the early 20th century was a genre of rock music called 'grunge'. This genre was characterised by a raw, unpolished guitar sound and screaming yet heartfelt vocals. Popular grunge artists included Nirvana, Pearl Jam and Mudhoney.

Activity 1

Below is an **introductory paragraph** for an informative web page about flying foxes. Unfortunately the sentences are out of order. Reorder these sentences from 1 to 4 to make the introductory paragraph correct.

______ Unfortunately, flying foxes are sometimes seen as pests, but in fact they are very interesting and important mammals.

______ Through their feeding they disperse the seeds of native plants.

______ Australia has four species of *Pteropus* flying fox.

______ In fact, flying foxes play a very important role in the environment.

Activity 2

Use the information below to write an **introductory paragraph** about Muhammad Ali.

- Born Cassius Marcellus Clay Jnr
- Converted to Islam in his 20s, and adopted the name Muhammad Ali
- Three-time World Heavyweight Champion and Olympic gold medallist
- His boxing style was famously captured in the line, 'Float like a butterfly, sting like a bee.'
- Ali's outgoing personality and his stance against war made him a controversial figure for many.

____

____

____

____

Activity 3

Write the **introductory paragraph** for your informative web page about a controversial historical figure.

Body paragraphs

The **body** of an informative **web page** consists of a series of paragraphs providing the most important and relevant information about a topic. Often the specific focus of each of the body paragraphs is identified via a **subheading**.

A subheading is a one- or two-word summary of the content of the paragraph and helps to organise information. For example, *Early life* could be the subheading for a paragraph summarising the events in the early life of the person who a web page is about.

Sometimes paragraphs are ordered from the most interesting information to the least interesting. However, if the web page topic is a historical event or figure, the paragraphs are ordered **chronologically**.

Activity 4

Put the subheadings below in the correct order, labelling them from 1 to 4. The topic is *Man landing on the moon*.

_____ The eagle has landed

_____ Back to Earth

_____ Blast off

_____ One giant leap for mankind

Activity 5

Write on the lines below the three or four **subheadings** you will use for your topic. Be sure to put them in order!

a ____________________

b ____________________

c ____________________

d ____________________

Activity 6

Read the example **body paragraph** below and then answer the questions.

The origins of the Dalai Lama are remarkable. Born in northeast Tibet to a peasant family, Lhamo Dhondup was only two years old when religious officials identified him as the reincarnation of the 13th Dalai Lama. Lhamo was the fifth of 16 children. It had taken the religious officials many months to find Lhamo. An important spiritual leader had a vision of where the next Dalai Lama resided, and led others to find him. When he was found, Lhamo was renamed Tenzin Gyatso and given the title of 14th Dalai Lama.

a Where was Lhamo Dhondup born? ____________________

b How many siblings did Dhondup have? ____________________

c What do you think is the most important piece of information in the paragraph?

____

d Which of the three subheadings would be best for this paragraph?

i Birth and death of the Dalai Lama

ii Finding the Dalai Lama

iii Living as the reincarnation of the 13th Dalai Lama

Activity 7

Choose one of the **subheadings** you identified in Activity 5 and write a draft **body paragraph** for that subheading.

Concluding paragraph

The **concluding paragraph** is a very short paragraph that **reviews** what has been written in the other paragraphs, and provides readers with a series of **hyperlinks** to find further information on the topic.

For example:
Ned Kelly remains a controversial figure, loved as a hero of the underdogs by some and despised as a ruthless killer by others. There are few Australian icons who have generated as much interest as Ned Kelly. To find out more about his story, visit one of the websites below:

www.ironoutlaw.com
www.oldmelbournegaol.com.au
www.glenrowantouristcentre.com.au
www.thekellytrail.com

Activity 8

Write your **concluding paragraph**.

You will need to use the internet to find three to five suitable websites with more information about your chosen historical event.

Language feature

Objective language

Informative websites are very common on the internet. People trust informative websites to provide information about issues and topics of interest. To focus on the information, and not the opinion or attitude of the writer, websites need to be written using **objective language**.

Objective language is **factual and free from bias, opinion and feelings**. Objective language avoids the use of highly emotive, exaggerated language and instead uses **neutral language**. Examples of objective words are *suspect, determine, estimate, report* and *indicate.*

An example of objective language:
Cyclist Lance Armstrong disappointed the public when he admitted to using steroids.

An example of biased, opinion-based language:
I was disgusted and disappointed by the appalling admission by Lance Armstrong that he took illegal steroids.

Activity 1

Identify whether the statements below are **fact** or **opinion**.

a Champion boxer Mike Tyson was sent to gaol for three years. ____________________

b Many of Pablo Picasso's works were politically motivated. ____________________

c I've never liked Madonna. ____________________

d Shakespeare's play *Hamlet* is the best piece of writing I've ever read. ____________________

e Tennis player John McEnroe is famous for his on-court tantrums. ____________________

f Woody Allen's films are weird and boring. ____________________

Activity 2

Remove feelings and opinion from the statements below by rewriting them in **objective language**.

a New Year's Day celebrations are brilliant and I enjoy them immensely, especially the stunning fireworks display on Sydney Harbour.

____

____

b Soccer is an absurd game because so many players fake injuries to get penalties.

____

____

c The idea that people play video games professionally is laughable.

____

____

d Mother Theresa was an amazing woman and is my inspiration to be a kind person every day.

____

____

Activity 3

Below is a list of sentences. Underline the words and phrases in each sentence that make it not objective. These words and phrases may be obvious statements of opinion (e.g. *I think*) or less obvious indications of an attitude or feeling (e.g. choice of adjective or adverb).

a In my opinion, there is no other innovator as important to the 21st century as Steve Jobs.

b My favourite sportsperson is the amazing and talented Muhammad Ali who fought against racial and religious prejudice.

c The outrageous fashion of singer Lady Gaga makes her a powerful idol for many young artists, including myself.

d I believe Michael Jackson's childhood was disturbed and led to his unhealthy obsession with people and objects in adulthood.

e The brave and intelligent American president Barack Obama challenged the old-fashioned attitudes and ideas of many Americans.

Frequently misspelt words

There are some words that are so often spelt incorrectly that they come to be known as **demons**. These words usually either are more difficult to sound out, have one particular part that is unusual or are an exception to a rule.

Strategies that you can use to help you spell these words include:

- **look, cover, spell, check**
- break the word into syllables.
  For example: *des–per–ate*
- use a **memory trick**—you can invent these for yourself
  For example: privilege has two eyes (i) and one leg (leg)
- **say the word out loud**— there is always at least one letter for each sound in a word so you will have a better chance of spelling it correctly.

Below is a list of frequently misspelt words:

accommodate
acknowledgment
adolescent
amateur
anxious
appreciate
approximately
because
category
conscious
definitely
desperate
embarrass
immediately
independent
lieutenant
literally
manoeuvre
miscellaneous
occasionally
privilege
separate
simultaneously
tragedy
transferred
tremendous

Study the words above using the *look, cover, spell, check* method. When you feel you are confident, cover them with a piece of paper and do the activities.

Activity 1

Underline the **correct spelling** in these word pairs.

- **a** adolesent/adolescent
- **b** tranfered/transferred
- **c** simultaneousely/simultaneously
- **d** immediately/immediatly
- **e** occasionally/ocasionally
- **f** desparate/desperate
- **g** approximately/approximatly
- **h** embarrass/embarass

Activity 2

Correct the words below. They are each missing a **syllable** or **sound**.

- **a** miscelleous ____________________
- **b** privlege ____________________
- **c** lieutnant ____________________
- **d** desprate ____________________
- **e** definely ____________________
- **f** apprecate ____________________
- **g** tremedous ____________________
- **h** litrally ____________________

Activity 3

Put a cross next to the sentences which contain spelling errors. Then write the corrections in the spaces.

a The filmmaker Alfred Hitchcock created a seperate genre of horror films.

____

b Woody Allen did not appresiate his films being put in the romantic comedy category.

____

c Social media tycoon Mark Zuckerberg argues that he has tried to accommodate for privacy in the latest version of Facebook. ____________________

d It is because of Lady Gaga that many women are less conscous of their appearance.

____

e The retiring prime minister thanked the other politicians for their acknowledgment of his contribution to Australian politics. ____________________

f His sudden death at the age of 36 was definately a tradgedy for the world.

____

g There is nothing more impressive than the maneouvers of motorcycle racing champion Casey Stoner. ____________________

h Even when Ali was still an amatuer boxer he was never anxious about his performance.

____

You be the teacher

Below is a **body paragraph** for a **web page** written by a Year 10 student. There are some errors in the structure of the paragraph and the spelling of some of the words. Can you correct the mistakes? Rewrite the paragraph with the **correct structure** and with the **correct spelling of all words**.

His interest in hi-hop started in his early teens and this was when he started using the name 'M&M', later to transfform into the stage name 'Eminem'. His early life was unstable, espeshully his adolesence, as he was brought up in a low-income, single-parent family in Michigan. Born Marshall Bruce Mathers III in October 1972, Eminem has emmerged as one of the most controvershal mushians of all time.

Now you write

It is now time for you to complete your own **web page** on a controversial figure.

1. Before you write, take some time to look at the student writing sample on the following page as a guide to writing standards.

2. Once you have read the student writing sample, take some time to think about what you believe are the most important features of an informative web page that you need to master. Use the lines below to jot down your answer to this question:
What do you find most difficult when writing this kind of text?

3. Now look at the informative marking criteria on page vii to double-check that you understand the requirements for a really good piece of informative writing.
Remember that you have already done your planning and drafted your introductory paragraph, one body paragraph and concluding paragraph. Use your own paper. Good luck!

Looking at other students' writing

Web pages:
Compose a web page about a popular video game franchise.

Introduction
The introduction alerts the audience to the topic of the web page in an interesting way.

Informative language
The student writes with clear and precise language. Third-person narrative is used to create an objective, factual tone.

Text structure
The student uses the correct structure for an informative web page: an introduction, body and conclusion.

Paragraphing
Each paragraph features detailed and appropriate information under subheadings.

ADVANCED SAMPLE

COMPOSE A WEB PAGE ABOUT A POPULAR VIDEO GAME FRANCHISE

It's unlikely that game designer Shigeru Miyamoto would have anticipated that his 1981 video game *Donkey Kong* would have been the beginning of a multimillion-dollar video game franchise. However, that's exactly what happened! Mario and his brother Luigi are probably the most recognisable video game characters in the world.

Origins of Mario

Mario first appeared in the arcade game *Donkey Kong*. In this game the protagonist was named 'Jump Man'. However, he eventually was renamed 'Mario' after Miyamoto's landlord. In this platformer game, Mario had to overcome a series of obstacles to defeat *Donkey Kong* and rescue 'Pauline'.

Plot and characters

The majority of the Mario video games follow the story of Mario and his brother Luigi as they attempt to rescue Princess Peach from the evil monster Bowser. This narrative was first developed in the side-scrolling *Super Mario* games. Mario and Luigi are plumbers who live in the Mushroom Kingdom. Characters that players frequently encounter in the Mario franchise are:

- Mario
- Bowser
- Yoshi
- Donkey Kong.
- Luigi
- Princess Peach
- Toad

Controversy

The Mario franchise has run into controversy in recent years regarding the representation of female characters, specifically Princess Peach. Well-known feminist theorist Anita Sarkeesian criticised the franchise for its representation of Princess Peach as a stereotypical 'damsel in distress'. She argued that the narrative of the games was too narrow. Responses to this critique highlight the fact that Princess Peach has her own spin-off game, Super Princess Peach, where she is the main protagonist of the game.

***

The Mario franchise has been successful since its origins in 1981 and, given the popularity of recent spin-off games, the franchise is likely to continue to be popular for many more years. To find out more, look at the links below:

The Mushroom Kingdom
The History of Super Mario Bros
The True Face of Mario

Vocabulary
Language is appropriate. Complex vocabulary is used where suitable for a web page, e.g. *protagonist*, *encounter*.

Sentence structure
A variety of simple, compound and complex sentences are used.

Ideas
Strong ideas that are relevant to the topic are included in each body paragraph. Ideas are detailed and well explained.

Cohesion
Each paragraph opens with a succinct topic sentence which matches the subheading. All paragraphs focus on the central topic of the web page: the Mario video game franchise.

Punctuation
Correct punctuation is used in the proposal.

Spelling
All words are spelt correctly, including technical and complex words.

UNIT NINE

Imaginative texts

Fan fiction stories

Understanding the question

Write a fan fiction story based on your favourite television show.

Type of question

This question is asking you to write a particular type of imaginative text—a **fan fiction story**.

The purpose of a short story is to **entertain** readers and **engage their emotions, imagination and thoughts**. Short stories are brief and so tend to focus on one character, setting and event. Fan fiction is a short story based on an existing original text.

You are being asked to write a short story based on a television show that you love.

Features of an opinion piece

- Aims to entertain the reader by adding to, or altering, the original works of others
- Develops original or appropriated (taken from another narrative) characters through dialogue, descriptions of actions and distinctive voices
- Has action occurring in a distinctive setting, which can be the same or different to that of the original work
- Has a structure composed of an orientation, complication and resolution
- Uses a variety of sentence structures: simple, compound and complex
- Has strong action verbs and emotive language
- Uses figurative language
- Uses first- or third-person narrative

1 This unit's question asks you to write a short story and tells you what to base it on. Define the three **content words** in this question.

a fan ____________________

b fiction ____________________

c story ____________________

2 Do a quick internet search and write a one-sentence definition of the term **fan fiction**.

____

____

The best fan fiction writers have a really good knowledge of the original texts they base their stories on. That's why it's important to carefully plan your story, to make sure you base it closely on the original text.

Planning and organisation

You must **plan** before every piece of writing you do. When planning for your short story you should:

- decide on the main **setting** and **character** for your story
- **plot the action** of your story using a plot graph.

Your story will be a fan fiction story based on your favourite television show.

1 **a** List your favourite television shows.

______________________ ______________________

______________________ ______________________

______________________ ______________________

b From your list above, select the television show that you feel most confident in writing your fan fiction story about. Remember: you need to know the show really well to be able to convincingly write a fan fiction story about it!

2 Using your knowledge of the television show you have selected, complete the table below.

Title of television show	
Main characters	
Main settings	
Genre of show	
Two-hundred-word summary of the television show's main plot	

It's important to note that there are **two different styles** of fan fiction.

Canon stories

These narratives **retain the world of the original text** (settings, characters and main plot) but change some elements of the plot such as the ending or add in additional scenes. For example: Changing the narrative of *Harry Potter and the Deathly Hallows* so house elf Dobby doesn't die.

Alternative universe stories

These narratives **place the characters from the original text into a new setting**, such as the setting from another original text.
For example: Putting the character Harry Potter into the world of *Lord of the Rings.*

Here are some possibilities for your fan fiction story:

- write what happens after an episode has ended
- write a scene from a minor character's perspective
- write the prequel or the sequel of the television show
- change a sequence of the narrative, e.g. a new character is introduced; a dead character is brought back to life; the characters are a different species, race or gender; or a new obstacle/conflict is introduced
- move a character from one narrative world to another
- change the setting or genre of the narrative.

3 Use the lines below to brainstorm ideas for a **canon** and an **alternative universe** story based on the television show you have chosen.

Canon story: ____________________

____

____

____

Alternative universe story: ____________________

____

____

4 It is now time to plan your story properly. Write answers to the questions below to help you fully plan your **fan fiction story**.

a What is the title of your original television show? ____________________

b Why did you choose this television show? ____________________

____

c What narrative elements (plot, characters, setting, theme and style) of the television show will you keep the same? ____________________

____

d Why did you decide to keep these narrative elements? ____________________

____

e What narrative elements will you change? ____________________

f Why did you decide to change these narrative elements? ____________________

____

g Who will be the main characters in your story? (Name and briefly describe them.)

____

h What will be the main settings in your story? (Name and briefly describe them.)

____

i What will be the main action of your story? Will there be conflict? How will the conflict be resolved?

____

____

j Would your fan fiction be best described as a canon story or an alternative universe story? Why?

____

____

____

Structure

Even though you're only writing part of a much larger, pre-existing narrative your story will still feature the structure of a traditional **narrative**: **orientation**, **complication** and **resolution**.

Orientation

This part of a short story is typically no longer than one or two paragraphs. In this section you **introduce your setting and your character**. A strong orientation will **grab the reader's attention** and make them want to keep reading. Creating action or intrigue can do this.

The orientation of a fan fiction story is slightly different to that of other short stories. Remember that your readers will probably have a good prior knowledge of the text your fan fiction is based on. That means you don't need to write a long back-story for your characters. If you're rewriting the end of an episode, you will need to briefly give some background to the action.

Below is an example of an orientation paragraph from a fan fiction story based on *Batman: Arkham Asylum*. Arkham Asylum is a psychiatric facility where the very worst, mentally unstable criminals in Gotham City are kept. Harley Quinn is the girlfriend of Batman's enemy The Joker and has become Batman's enemy as well. Robin is Batman's sidekick:

'Wake up, Bird-Boy!'

Robin woke up, slowly rose to his feet, and wiped his forehead. He had blood running down his face, forming a pool where he had been lying. He looked up and realised he was trapped in a small, prison-like cell. Harley Quinn was on the outside of the cell, walking back and forth, tapping a crowbar along the cell bars. Harley normally looked fairly innocent, despite how evil she was, but Robin could tell she was angry. Very angry.

(By Daniel Mills)

Activity 1

Carefully read the example **orientation** paragraph above, then tick those techniques that have been used to engage the readers from the list given below.

* detail of a character's thoughts
* detailed description of a place
* mix of sentence lengths
* figurative language
* dialogue
* action verbs
* extended dialogue

Activity 2

Using your own paper, write the **orientation** paragraphs of your fan fiction story.

Complication

Conflict happens in all stories, including fan fiction. Conflict makes life complicated, which is why this part of the story is called the **complication**. Will your story feature a conflict from the original narrative, or will you introduce a new conflict?

Activity 3

Below is an example of a paragraph introducing the **conflict** in a fan fiction story based on the novel *Looking for Alaska* by John Green. The novel focuses on the story of Miles Halter who falls in love with the enigmatic Alaska Young and tries to unravel the mystery of her past.

The paragraph below from the fan fiction based on *Looking for Alaska* is jumbled. Use the numbers 1 to 4 to correctly order the four sections.

______ I didn't want him to know that I was terrified it was about Alaska.
"Not sure."
The Eagle began talking.

______ Some faces I recognised and a lot I didn't. I found a seat on the bleachers next to Takumi and the Colonel.

______ I finally made it down to the gym with everyone else. I was the last to enter. Everyone from the entire campus was squashed into one room.

______ "Hey Pudge. Where you been?" Without even waiting for my answer, he kept talking, "What do you think this is all about?"

(By Kristi Vanderfield)

Activity 4

Using your own paper, write one paragraph from the **complication** section of your fan fiction story. Remember to look back through your planning notes on the previous pages, as you have already considered what the action of your story will be.

Resolution

This is the part of the story where the **problem is overcome and life begins to return to normal**. Many stories include a final scene called a **coda** where the character reflects on their experience and the lesson learned.

Think carefully about the episode of your favourite television show that you have chosen to base your story on. How is the narrative's conflict resolved? Does the bad guy get caught? Do the main characters fall in love? Is the lost child found?

Some questions to consider before drafting your story's resolution are:

- will you change or keep the original narrative's ending?
- why have you decided this?

Activity 5

Write some notes about the **resolution** to your fan fiction story. This may take the form of a draft or a few dot points. Use your own paper to draft this paragraph.

Language feature

Symbolism

A symbol is an **object that represents an abstract idea, emotion, action or event**. Symbols are **figurative** (non-literal) and can be seen as a complicated form of **metaphor**. It is important to note that symbols can change meaning due to the context in which they are used. For example, the word *chain* might represent unity in one context but represent imprisonment in another.

For example:

broken glass = bad luck
shadow = mystery
rain = sadness
candle = hope
light bulb = innovation or new idea
dove = peace

Symbolism is the use of symbols to signify ideas and qualities by giving them meaning different to their literal meaning. There are two main types of symbolism: **everyday symbolism** and **literary symbolism**.

Everyday symbolism is the use of symbols in everyday life that we encounter frequently without even knowing it. Symbolism is used often in advertising, fashion, the celebration of occasions and in the interaction between people.

For example:

handshake = respect
smile = friendship
heart shape = love
sunflowers = happiness
diamond = eternity

Activity 1

Match the **everyday symbol** with what it represents.

a roses	royalty
b crown	romance
c black	death
d skull	evil
e dollar sign	new beginning
f sunrise	money

Literary symbolism is when **everyday symbols are used in works of literature to represent a complex or hidden idea**. Writers use symbolism when they want to express an idea without explicitly saying it. Symbols in stories can help to create a specific mood or emotion. For example, a storm may symbolise impending chaos or grief for a character in a story. Some symbols are obvious, but others are subtle and hidden.

Activity 2

In the sentences below, a **symbol** has been underlined. Read the sentences carefully and then use the given lines to explain what the symbol represents.

a I stepped silently towards her holding a single red rose in my hand.

____

b 'My heart leaps up when I behold / A rainbow in the sky.'

____

c 'About midnight, while we still sat up, the storm came rattling over the Heights in full fury.'

____

d 'But the stars were shining beyond the mist, and the moon was coming, and the evening was not dark.'

____

e 'Move him into the sun / Gently its touch awoke him once / At home, whispering of fields unsown.'

____

Spotlight *on spelling*

Apostrophes

An **apostrophe** can be used for two reasons:

- to show **possession**
- to show that a word has been **contracted**.

In this unit, we will be focusing on the use of apostrophes to show contractions. The word **contraction** in this context simply means to **bring two words together to make one word**. The apostrophe shows that letters from the original words are missing.

In a contraction, the apostrophe always goes in the spot where the missing letters would have been.

For example:

what is → what's   can not → can't

Look at the following examples of how contractions are formed.

- The word *not* is contracted when used with the verbs *have, has, is, does, were, would, are, can* and *could*.

  For example:

  could + not → couldn't   can + not → can't   would + not → wouldn't

  do + not → don't   will + not → won't

- Single words can be made from a pronoun such as *he, she, they, it, I, we* and *you*, and a contracted form of the word *will*.

  For example:

  she + will → she'll   he + will → he'll

  they + will → they'll   we + will → we'll

* Single words can be made from a pronoun and a contracted form of the verb *to be*. The verb *be* includes the words *are, is* and *am*.

  For example:

he + is → he's	she + is → she's
we + are → we're	I + am → I'm

  Note: The contractions for *has* and *is* are the same (*'s*) so the meaning will depend on the context.

  For example: She's finished her book (she has).
  She's in the kitchen. (she is)

  Take special note of the following four contractions:

who + is → who's	you + are → you're
it + is → it's	they + are → they're

  The contractions above are often confused with their homophones, shown below.

who's and *whose*	*you're* and *your*
it's and *its*	*they're* and *their/there*

* Single words can be made from a pronoun or a modal verb and a contracted form of the verb *have*. The verb *have* includes the words *have* and *has*.

  For example:

I + have → I've	he + has → he's
you + have → you've	we + have → we've
would + have → would've	should + have → should've

* Single words can be made from a pronoun and the contracted form of *would* or *had*. However, the contraction for both *would* and *had* is the same (*'d*) so the meaning of the contraction will depend on the context.

I'd — I had/I would	he'd — he had/he would
she'd — she had/she would	it'd — it had/it would
you'd — you had/you would	we'd — we had/we would
they'd — they had/they would	

  For example: They'd never been there before. (they had)
  They'd like to return soon. (they would)

* Finally, verbs can be contracted with nouns to create new words.

  For example:
  Fred + will → Fred'll
  Fred'll be leaving at 8 pm.

  Mum + is → Mum's
  Mum's working tomorrow.

  Lee + has → Lee's
  Lee's been studying hard.

  girl + is → girl's
  That tall girl's the faster player.

  Note: the apostrophe followed by *s* is also used to show possession (e.g. *Keenan's bicycle*—the bicycle of Keenan). So always think about what the apostrophe is showing when you read a word containing one, and always think about whether you need one and why.

Activity 1

Correct any incorrect spellings in the sentences below.

a There arent many people who can get away with having bright pink hair. ______________________

b Thats the last time I let my younger brother choose the movie! ______________________

c Why isnt' chocolate healthy? I'd eat it all day long if it was. ______________________

d Sarah and Monique do'nt enjoy being stared at when walking down the street. ______________________

e They were pleased that there new baby was a boy. ______________________

f Who's phone is this one? ______________________

g Inside the trunk of the dark oak tree was Balins special hiding place. ______________________

Activity 2

Write the correct **contraction** for each set of words. Then choose the correct contraction from the list to complete the sentences below. There may be more than one possibility.

did not	______________________	they will	______________________
they would	______________________	he would	______________________
were not	______________________	has not	______________________
had not	______________________	who is	______________________
I have	______________________	we have	______________________
he will	______________________	they had	______________________
would have	______________________	it is	______________________
you are	______________________	they are	______________________

a ______________________ been waiting for three years for their daughter to return.

b They think ______________________ going to rain before they arrive.

c Do you think ______________________ done enough to achieve A's?

d Lilly ______________________ arrived on time but her car broke down.

e The men ______________________ feel confident that their gear would last the trip.

f Huo ______________________ bought his ticket for the movie because he doesn't have the money.

g ______________________ been patient with him in the past; today I am feeling less kind.

You be the teacher

Below is a **body paragraph** for a fan fiction story written by a Year 10 student. There are some errors in the structure of the paragraph and the spelling of some of the words using **apostrophes** to show **contractions**. Can you correct the mistakes? Rewrite the paragraph with the **correct structure** and with the **correct spelling of all words**.

As she bent, her ginger hair fell softly over her eyes. After all, no one else was willing to devote their lives to solving the mysteries hidden deep in the X Files. Scully bent down to look closely at the small, oddly shaped footprints pressed lightly into the damp soil. This slight movement was'nt dramatic, yet it made Mulder's heart beat a tiny bit faster than it shouldv'e. He turned away, bringing his eyes to the same prints Scully was now intently measuring. They mustnt be distracted from the task at hand.

Now you write

It is now time for you to complete your own **fan fiction story** based on your favourite television show.

1 Before you write, take some time to look at the student writing sample on the following page as a guide to writing standards.

2 Once you have read the student writing sample, take some time to think about what you believe are the most important features of a fan fiction story that you need to master.
Use the space below to jot down your answer to this question:
What do you find most difficult when writing this kind of text?

3 Now look at the imaginative text marking criteria on page viii to double-check that you understand the requirements for a really good piece of imaginative writing.

Remember that you have already done your planning and drafted your orientation and a complication paragraph, and written notes for your resolution. Use your own paper. Good luck!

Looking at other students' writing

Fan fiction stories:

Write a fan fiction story based on your favourite novel.

ADVANCED SAMPLE

WRITE A FAN FICTION STORY BASED ON YOUR FAVOURITE NOVEL.

Note: This fan fiction story is based on the novel *Looking for Alaska* by John Green.

Later that night

Skin and bones. That's all she was. A pile of skin and bones being kept alive by machines. No light blue toenails, no intense eyes, no sweet smell of raspberries and cigarettes. It was like someone had ripped out everything that made her Alaska and left the other pieces to rot.

It took me 4 hours and 28 minutes to work up the courage to enter her room, but all the time in the world wouldn't have made what I saw any easier. She was unresponsive all night but I still waited for her to say something until one of the nurses came in at exactly 9:01 and told me visiting hours were over and that I needed to leave. So I sat in the waiting room and just waited.

I waited for tomorrow.
I waited for the sun to slowly rise.
I waited for the nurses to start their shifts and others to finish theirs.
I waited until breakfast was over.
Then I waited for Alaska to wake up.

Two days later

At 8:00 am visiting hours began and I walked back to campus. I started to get mad at Alaska. Mad at her for making me a promise she had little intention of keeping. Mad at her for changing me and then leaving.

'YOU CAN'T JUST MAKE ME DIFFERENT AND THEN LEAVE!' I shouted out into emptiness. No one was on the dirt road I walked along. No one could hear me. Not Alaska. No one. But quite frankly I don't think she'd care anyway.

Maybe deep down I knew it was the end for her and maybe I was too scared to do something. I was mad at myself for not realising how deeply unhappy she was earlier.

I made it back to campus at 10:00 am. I didn't care about getting caught by the Eagle because all I cared about was Alaska.

Eight days later

Alaska never woke up. No amount of time could've fixed every broken part of her.

When Alaska's father found out about her accident he immediately came into town and stayed with her unresponsive body for the entire time. Yesterday she started getting worse and her father had no choice but to let her go, just as I had that night.

As much as I wanted to hate Alaska, I couldn't. She helped me to find my *great perhaps*, and she tore me apart into a million pieces but I don't think I would have had it any other way. I had hoped one day she would tell her kids about me, about the time we pranked the Eagle so badly or the sticky hot day we met. But all that is gone, all I have left is the smell of her that will slowly fade, and countless days to forgive her for the way she left me.

I think we're both to blame for how things ended and I have to be okay with that. Alaska is probably better off wherever she is now, so I know she forgives me, just as I forgive her.

Introduction
A strong orientation grabs the reader's attention through the use of intrigue.

Narrative techniques
Descriptive language engages the reader's imagination. Sensory imagery is effective. Repetition of *I waited* exaggerates the protagonist's agony.

Text structure
The fan fiction is well structured, featuring an obvious orientation, complication and resolution.

Paragraphing
A new paragraph is used to introduce each new main part of the story's action. Tension is built effectively.

Vocabulary
Complex vocabulary is used, e.g. *intentions* and *unresponsive*. A variety of strong adjectives and verbs are used to enhance the images created, e.g. *intense, ripped out, rot* and *countless*.

Sentence structure
A variety of sentence lengths is used to avoid monotony and create interest. Short sentences create drama. Some sentence fragments (phrases and incomplete sentences) are used with good narrative effect, e.g. *Skin and bones, Not Alaska, No one*.

Ideas
The theme of the short story (loss and grief) is developed and sustained throughout.

Cohesion
There is continuity of ideas throughout the description —the focus is always on Miles's grief at losing Alaska.

Punctuation
Correct punctuation is used. Complex punctuation is used where required.

Spelling
All words are spelt correctly, including some difficult and challenging words, e.g. *immediately, emptiness* and *intention*.

UNIT TEN

10

Imaginative texts

Protest poems

Understanding the question

Compose a poem that protests against bullying.

Type of question

This question is asking you to write a particular type of imaginative text—a **protest poem**.

How do you know a protest poem is required? The verb *protests* and the topic of bullying are the clues. A protest poem is a lot like other poems, in that it aims to evoke an **emotional response** from the reader. Many protest poems are intended to be read aloud to an audience. This affects the choices the poet makes about structure and language.

Features of a protest poem

- Aims to stimulate an emotional response about a social problem like war or racism
- Encourages listeners to take action about a social problem
- Is very persuasive and emotive
- Is usually written subjectively
- Features a strong, passionate voice
- Uses a range of poetic devices
- Can be written in free verse or tightly structured

1 Identify the two **content words** in the question and define each one.

2 **Protest poems** aim to raise awareness of social problems. Identify five social problems that poets might write about.

Planning and organisation

A **protest poem** is a piece of writing that aims to inform and persuade. It also aims to evoke strong emotions in the reader. Before you can begin writing your poem, you need to do some **thinking** and **research** about the topic your poem will be about—bullying.

TIP

Writing a great poem takes many attempts. Don't be surprised if you spend a lot of time on your drafts!

Activity 1

Use your own knowledge as well as internet research to complete the table below.

Types of bullying	Causes of bullying	Effects of bullying	Possible solutions to bullying

Activity 2

Voice is very important when writing a protest poem. Deciding whose perspective on an issue you will give voice to is hard and depends on your own personal attitude towards the issue. A number of people are involved in bullying: the bully, the victim, school teachers, parents, friends and bystanders.

In the table below, brainstorm the types of voices each of these people may have. You might like to use a series of **adjectives** such as *harsh*, *angry*, *soft* or *sad*. You should also add a brief description of what their attitude towards bullying might be. The first one has been done for you as a guide.

Person	Attitude	Voice
bully	enjoys being the centre of attention, thinks the victim is weak, is angry with the world and needs to vent this	aggressive, sarcastic, uncaring
victim		
friend		
bystander		
teacher		
parent		

Structure

A **protest poem** can be structured in many different ways. It may be written in **free verse**, with no obvious rhythm or rhyme and without any obvious stanzas. It might be **highly structured**, with strong **rhythm** and **rhyme** and divided into even-length **stanzas**.

For this task, you are going to write a poem with regular **metre**. You will learn more about metre on page 101.

Often protest poems tell a story of someone who has suffered as a result of some form of **social injustice**. Examples of social injustice include racism, prejudice, bullying and sexism. Poets also write protest poems about bigger **problems that affect mankind** such as war, poverty, pollution and consumerism.

You will be writing a poem about a social justice issue—bullying. You may wish to have your poem structured like a narrative, with an orientation, complication or resolution, or it might be written as a series of different images or voices relating to the issue of bullying.

Here are some ideas for how to approach the writing of your poem:

- adopt a tone of defiance
- adopt the voice of the bully
- ask a series of provocative questions
- adopt the voice of the victim.

You should **avoid writing a hate poem** that is overly aggressive or negative. The better protest poems are those which are subtle and rely on suggestion. A great protest poem will have a careful balance between emotion and facts.

Below are two stanzas from a poem protesting against the prejudice people with disabilities face in society.

Activity 1

Read the two stanzas below and then answer the following questions.

When he is wrongly judged next time,
I will show them they're not right.
My words put together so sublime,
I shall tell them of his plight.

Changing the mind of just one person
Can change the mind of many,
It can better not worsen
His happiness, worth the same as any.

a Who is the speaker of the poem?

____

b What tone of voice does the speaker use?

____

c What line do you think is the most powerful? Why?

____

Activity 2

Complete the sentences below.

My poem will be ________ lines long.

The speaker in my poem will be ____

I have chosen this speaker because ____

____

The mood of my poem will be ____

I will create this mood by ____

____

Activity 3

Using your own paper, draft the first four lines of your poem.

Using a regular rhythm (metre) in your poem will be tricky. You will need to play around with the arrangement of words. This is why poetry sometimes reads like Yoda has written it!

Language feature

Metre

Metre is the **pattern of stressed and unstressed beats** in a line of poetry. The length of lines of poetry varies, depending on the number of feet in the line. A **foot** in a line of poetry is a **small group of syllables**, typically two or three syllables. Some syllables in a foot are stressed and some are unstressed. A stressed syllable is one that has **added emphasis** to it, and an unstressed syllable is spoken more softly.

Here we will focus on two main types of metre—**iambic** and **trochaic**—as they are the type of metre you are most likely to use in your protest poem. An **annotating key** will help you identify the stressed and unstressed syllables in each foot. We will use **x** for unstressed and **/** for stressed. Don't be concerned if this doesn't make sense straight away, because there is a bit of counting which makes it more like Maths!

In **iambic metre**, the first syllable is unstressed and the second is stressed.

(Note: in each example below, the lines have been broken into their feet to better indicate the metre. The stressed syllables have also been put in **bold** font.)

x / x / x / x / x /
My **mist**|ress' **eyes** |are **no**|thing **like** |the **sun**

(William Shakespeare, *Sonnet 130*)

In **trochaic metre**, the first syllable is stressed and the second is unstressed.

/ x / x / x
Little |**Lamb**, who |**made** thee?

(William Blake, *The Lamb*)

When using either of these metres, the line lengths may vary, but the combination of stressed and unstressed beats (known as 'feet') will remain.

Below are some examples of varying line lengths that use either iambic or trochaic metre. The technical names for each are given in brackets.

Example one:
I do not want to go to school again. (iambic pentameter)

Example two:
Black night, black night, go now. (trochaic trimeter)

Example three:
Inside the cave I am alone. (iambic tetrameter)

Example four:
Go now, away! (trochaic dimeter)

When naming the metre of a poem, you must first identify the type of metre and then the number of feet per line. For example, in the line below, the type of metre is iambic because the rhythm alternates between unstressed and stressed beats every two syllables. It is a pentameter because there are five sets of iambs. We therefore call this iambic pentameter.

x / x / x / x / x /
My **mist**|ress' **eyes** |are **no**|thing **like** |the **sun**
(William Shakespeare, *Sonnet 130*)

This list of the names given to the different line lengths will help you identify the type of metre used. Remember that **a foot is two beats**. An iamb is a single unit of rhythmic measurement that consists of an unstressed and a stressed syllable.

dimeter	two feet	hexameter	six feet
trimeter	three feet	heptameter	seven feet
tetrameter	four feet	octameter	eight feet
pentameter	five feet		

Activity 1

Using the information above about **metre**, answer the questions below.

a How many unstressed then stressed beats are in every line of iambic tetrameter? ________

b How many stressed then unstressed beats are in every line of trochaic octameter? ________

c How many feet are in every line of iambic dimeter? ________

d How many feet are in every line of trochaic heptameter? ________

Activity 2

Annotate the lines below with the **x** and / method to identify the **unstressed and stressed syllables**. You will need to read the lines aloud to do this. Using this information, identify what type of metre is being used in each line.The first one has been done for you.

x / x /
a That girl, that girl.
iambic dimeter

b You fool! You brute! You selfish farce! ________________

c Sing it softly, sing it loudly. ________________

d The birds fall from the shattered sky. ________________

Activity 3

Match the lines with the type of **metre** they have used.

trochaic pentameter	Don't step too fast.
iambic hexameter	Join hands, rise up, the time to fight is now.
iambic dimeter	The pain which they all feel but I do not wish to feel.
trochaic tetrameter	Are we just birds screeching away?

Finally, it is important to remember that the most important elements of a really good protest poem are **creativity** and **passion**. You will probably find that metre comes naturally to you, as we often speak in patterns without realising. Don't let your focus on metre interfere with the expression of your thoughts and feelings.

Activity 4

It's now time to draft one or two of the stanzas of your **protest poem** about bullying. Use your own paper for this activity.

Spotlight *on spelling*

Doubling the consonant before adding *ing*

Often protest poems are written in the **present tense**, as this gives a poem a sense of immediacy and urgency. When you write in the present tense, you will usually need to use **verbs ending in the suffix *ing***. This creates the present participle form of the word. Unfortunately, it is not always as easy as just adding *ing* to the root word—some words require you to double the final consonant before adding the suffix.

If the last three letters of a root verb consist of a consonant, single vowel and another consonant (such as **plan**) then you double the final consonant and add *ing*, so *plan* becomes *plann**ing***.

For example:
sit + *ing* → sitt**ing**
shut + *ing* → shutt**ing**
get + *ing* → gett**ing**

In two-syllable root verbs where the second syllable consists of a consonant, single vowel and another consonant, and where the stress is on **the second syllable**, we double the last consonant before adding *ing*.

For example:
permit + *ing* → permitt**ing**
refer + *ing* → referr**ing**
prefer + *ing* → preferr**ing**
regret + *ing* → regrett**ing**
defer + *ing* → deferr**ing**
forget + *ing* → forgett**ing**

If however the stress is on the **first syllable**, we do not double the final consonant.

For example:
happen + *ing* → happen**ing**
listen + *ing* → listen**ing**
offer + *ing* → offer**ing**
visit + *ing* → visit**ing**

Exception:

If the verb ends with a consonant, vowel and then the letter *l*, double the *l* and add *ing*, even if the stress is on the first syllable.

For example:

travel + *ing* → travel**ling**

marvel + *ing* → marvel**ling**

cancel + *ing* → cancel**ling**

We **never double** if there are already two consonants at the end of the verb, so *disgust* becomes *disgust***ing** and *repent* becomes *repent***ing**.

We **never double** if there are two vowels in a single root verb (e.g. *foam* becomes *foam***ing**) or if there are two vowels in the second syllable of the root verb (e.g. *derail* becomes *derail***ing**).

Activity 1

Using the rules above to guide you, add the suffix ***ing*** to the verbs below.

You may need to revise the spelling rules you learnt in Unit 7.

a watch ______________ **b** swim ______________

c hop ______________ **d** admit ______________

e scatter ______________ **f** pan ______________

g bar ______________ **h** arrive ______________

i date ______________ **j** damage ______________

k recycle ______________

Activity 2

Change the words below from the **past tense** to the **present participle**. The first one has been done for you.

a echoed ___echoing___ **b** rained ______________

c encompassed ______________ **d** flattened ______________

e evaded ______________ **f** travelled ______________

g shipped ______________ **h** hoped ______________

i listened ______________ **j** blotted ______________

k cleansed ______________ **l** chatted ______________

m faded ______________

You be the teacher

Below is a **stanza** for a protest poem written by a Year 10 student. There are some errors in the metre and spelling of words ending in *ing*. Can you correct the mistakes? Rewrite the stanza with the correct **metre** and **spelling**. You may need to add and/or omit words to achieve the correct metre.

Hint: the majority of the poem is written in **iambic tetrameter**.

Images haunt me really late at night,
Breakking my sleep with fright.
Stoping my shallow breathing
Are pictures of their deaths.

Now you write

It is now time for you to complete your own **protest poem** about bullying.

1 Before you write, take some time to look at the student writing sample on the following page as a guide to writing standards.

2 Once you have read the student writing sample, take some time to think about what you believe are the most important features of a protest poem that you need to master. Use the lines below to jot down your answer to this question:
What do you find most difficult when writing this kind of text?

3 Now look at the imaginative text marking criteria on page viii to double-check that you understand the requirements for a really good piece of imaginative writing.

Remember that you have already done your planning and drafted the first four lines of your poem. Use your own paper. Good luck!

Looking at other students' writing

Protest poems:

Write a protest poem about whaling.

Opening stanza
The first stanza grabs the reader's attention through the use of figurative language. The subject is clear though not specifically named.

Poetic techniques
Descriptive language engages the reader's imagination and emotions.

Sound devices such as alliteration and rhyme are used well. Metre is used consistently throughout.

Poem structure
The protest poem is structured as a series of images of the whales, the whalers and the conservationists' boat.

A new stanza is used to introduce each new idea or image of whaling.

ADVANCED SAMPLE

WRITE A PROTEST POEM ABOUT WHALING.

Far out into the deep, dark sea,
Is where the gentle giants will be.
Far down there they entertain,
No sadness, fear and no pain.

Silently stalking its sole prey,
A brutish boat of iron grey.
Weapons pointing from its strong side,
The precious whales they fail to hide.

The swift missile-like harpoon hits
Sending the whale into death's pit.
A sorrowful song of whale cries,
A carcass on the ship now lies.

Our heroes emerge from behind,
Unsure what horror they will find.
Bloody swirls stain the distressed sea,
No words convey their misery.
Grandest beings in our ocean,
Desperately need our protection.
Whale Saviours are the whales' true friend,
Fighting for the slaughter to end.

Vocabulary
Strong, vivid language is used to enhance the images created, e.g. *stalking, brutish, precious, sorrowful* and *carcass.*

Metre
Iambic tetrameter is maintained throughout. This rhyme pattern is well suited to the protest poem and theme.

Ideas
The theme of the protest poem (against whaling) is developed and sustained throughout.

Cohesion
There is continuity of ideas throughout the poem—the focus is always on the nature or causes of whaling.

Punctuation
There is appropriate use of commas and full stops at the end of lines.

Spelling
All words are spelt correctly.

UNIT ELEVEN

Imaginative texts
Genre short stories

Understanding the question

Write a short horror story.

Type of question

This question is asking you to write a type of imaginative text—a **genre short story**.

The purpose of a short story is to **entertain readers** and **engage their emotions, imagination and thoughts**. Short stories are brief and so tend to focus on one character, setting and event.

You are being asked to write a specific type of short story—a horror story. Horror is a type of **narrative genre**, and this question requires you to write using the conventions of the horror genre. The word genre can also refer to broad groupings of texts such as persuasive, informative and imaginative. However, in this task the word *genre* refers to particular types of narratives such as crime or science fiction.

Features of a genre short story

- Aims to entertain, with each genre also having its own particular aim; for example, horror stories aim to shock or scare their readers whereas science fiction stories aim to help people imagine different worlds
- Features an orientation, complication and resolution
- Adheres to generic conventions; for example, fantasy stories often feature a magical system, a hero and a quest
- Consists of a variety of sentence structures (simple, compound and complex)
- Uses strong action verbs and emotive and figurative language
- Written in first-person narrative or third-person narrative

1 What does the word ***horror*** mean?

____

2 List as many **genres** as you can in the space below.

____

____

3 From the list above, choose your five favourite **genres**. Put them in order from most favourite to least favourite.

____

____

____

Planning and organisation

The trick with writing really good **genre stories** is to discover the **conventions** of that genre. You can do this by reading and watching a range of texts in the genre, or by researching the genre online. This will give you a solid sense of what key elements must be included to ensure your story can be classified as horror, fantasy, science fiction, etc.

Activity 1

Below is a list of five **horror conventions**. For each convention, try to give an example from a film, novel, video game or play that you know.

- Settings are usually remote, ancient, abandoned or haunted.

- Characters include the supernatural (ghosts, vampires, werewolves), the mentally unstable (mad scientist) or an out-of-control human creation (Frankenstein's monster, robots).

- The main conflict often centres on a fight between good and evil, reason and the supernatural, or the dead and the living.

- The stories are designed to frighten, cause panic and create discomfort.

- The stories are frequently Gothic in style. Common features include ruined castles, storms, dream sequences, amulets or charms, darkness, fog or some type of evil presence such as a witch, vampire or demon.

Activity 2

Write a list of five **horror stories** that you know. These might be movies, books, poems or video games. For each one, briefly describe what, in particular, makes it a scary story.

a __________

b __________

c __________

d __________

e __________

Activity 3

We are all scared of something. Write a paragraph describing in detail what scares you the most.

Settings

The **setting** of a story is the **location** or locations **where the action takes place**. Horror stories are meant to scare people and have them question what they know about themselves, others and their world. Settings for these stories are usually spooky.

Activity 4

What are five **settings** typical of horror stories (e.g. haunted houses)?

Characters

All horror stories will have an **antagonist** and a **protagonist**. The protagonist is the hero or 'good guy' of a story. The antagonist is the enemy or 'bad guy' of a story.

Activity 5

Below is a list of ten different **characters** typical of horror stories.

a Identify which characters would be classified as **protagonists** and which as **antagonists**.

b Add two **characters** of your own to the list on the given lines. Identify whether they are likely to be antagonists or protagonists.

ghost		butcher	
vampire		teenager	
little girl		witch	
bride		scientist	
writer		zombie	

Activity 6

Use the table below to plan the **characters** and **setting** for your horror story. Remember to stick to the conventions you identified above.

Characters	Setting

Structure

Like all short stories, **genre stories** typically adhere to the **traditional narrative structure**. However, some genres subvert this structure. For example, often with the crime fiction genre, the main conflict or complication (e.g. murder or robbery) has already occurred so, in a way, the story starts in the middle. A horror story, however, usually features the following fairly traditional structure:

- the hero discovers something unusual
- the hero is given or accepts the task of investigating the unusual event or phenomenon
- the hero discovers that these events are truly happening
- the hero tries to stop the events, usually while trying to protect or save an innocent person (often a loved one)
- the hero tries to overcome or end the events or phenomena, or defeat the villain. The hero usually succeeds (but not always).

A great horror story will have a **theme**. A theme is the main message or idea that the writer would like to communicate to the reader. Sometimes it might seem that the only purpose of a horror story is to scare the reader, but horror stories often have quite serious themes underlying the scary narrative. Below are some common themes found in horror stories:

- fear of the unknown
- always stay hopeful
- life is full of despair
- love conquers all
- good will always triumph over evil
- faith wins the day
- there will always be mysteries in our world.

Subvert means 'challenge or overthrow conventions or rules'.

Activity 1

What **theme** would you like to explore in your horror story?

____

____

Orientation

Think of an **exciting opening sentence**. Your very first sentence needs to hook readers' interest to keep them reading. Try one of these types of story openers:

- dialogue between characters
- internal monologue of main character
- description of eerie location
- short action-packed sentences
- narrator starting the story at the beginning of events.

Activity 2

Match the examples below to their type of **opener**.

a Dialogue between characters	**i** I turned the corner. Nothing. Panting, I ran the opposite way. A green door appeared to my right. Bang!
b Internal monologue of main character	**ii** The wind whispered through the sparse trees, whipping dead leaves into the icy air.
c Description of eerie location	**iii** The possibility of losing Aimee is too hard to imagine. Each time I picture her in there with that haggard witch, my insides squirm.
d Narrator starts story at beginning of events	**iv** 'Where?' I ask quietly. 'In there, behind the bookshelf,' she hisses in my direction.
e Short action-packed sentences	**v** I first saw Dunwich Manor on a cold and dark Halloween Eve.

Activity 3

Who will be the **hero** of your story?

____

What must we know about your hero? Briefly describe the hero.

____

____

How will this subtly be revealed to the reader? Give concrete examples.

____

____

____

____

How much will you reveal in your orientation? Give concrete examples.

____

____

____

____

Activity 4

Write the **orientation** for your horror story.

____

____

____

____

____

Complication

Once you have orientated your readers with the setting and the main characters, it is time to introduce the **complication**. The complication typically involves some type of **conflict**.

Remember that the nature of conflict can be varied. You may have more than one conflict. Think about what type of conflict(s) your story will have:

- man vs man
- man vs environment
- man vs society
- man vs self
- man vs supernatural.

Horror stories may feature any one of the above types of conflict.

For example:

Man vs man: Freddy Krueger trying to kill teenage girls in their sleep

Man vs environment: evil monkeys attacking people

Man vs supernatural: vampire zombies in *I Am Legend*

Man vs self: the father goes insane in *The Shining*

Man vs society: the scientist fights against other citizens in *The Thing*

Activity 5

Below are brief descriptions of conflicts found in horror stories. For each one, identify which type of **conflict** it is. Use the list above to help with this task.

a A young girl falls into a swamp. ________________

b Three people battle a town of zombies. ________________

c A father tries to deal with the death of his son. ________________

d An axe-murderer chases a teenage boy. ________________

Typically, the **complication** of a horror story will involve the following events:

- the hero is given or accepts the task of investigating the unusual event or phenomenon
- the hero discovers that the events are truly happening
- the hero tries to stop the events, usually while trying to protect and save an innocent person (often a loved one).

You may like to follow this narrative structure, or you may wish to change some aspects of it.

Activity 6

Now that you have found out more about the complications often found in horror stories, it is time to begin drafting the **complication** paragraphs of your own story. Use your own paper for this task.

Resolution

Add a twist! The **ending of a horror story shouldn't be predictable**. Your job as the writer is to keep your readers guessing and then surprise them at the end! How will you do this? You may choose to leave the ending of your narrative incomplete—such as a **cliffhanger**—or you may make it an **unhappy ending**. Perhaps the bad guy might get away, or the good guy might die or lose loved ones. Of course, you might end the story happily, but the hero might save the day in a **surprising or unconventional** way. For example, instead of scaring away a ghost, maybe the hero becomes friends with the ghost.

Usually in horror stories the resolution is very **action-packed**. Not much time, if any, is spent on reflecting on lessons learned or how things turned out.

Activity 7

Below are summaries of the endings of three different stories. Match each **ending** with the correct type.

a	A father loses his daughter to demonic possession.	**i**	cliffhanger
b	A zombie vampire escapes.	**ii**	happy
c	The unhappy ghost of a woman is reunited with her husband.	**iii**	unhappy

Activity 8

Write the **resolution** to your horror story. Use your own paper for this task.

Language feature

Dialogue

Dialogue is the **conversation between characters** in a story. It is important that you use dialogue effectively. It should be used to reveal more about the **characters** or the **plot**.

Activity 1

For each of the examples of **dialogue** below, state whether the dialogue reveals more about the **characters** or more about the **plot**.

a 'My eyeballs feel like sandpaper and my legs haven't stopped aching for two hours.'

____

b 'Are you serious? We can't go in there! That's the vampire's lair. We're sure to be killed.'

____

c 'Whatever he says, I know that he still wants to avenge Alana's murder. There's no way he's going to let the creature escape.'

____

d 'Beth, this is likely to be the last chance that I will have to tell you this. I was wrong. We should never have followed that trail. I just needed to let you know. I'm sorry.'

____

e 'It's taken control of all communications. We should never have doubted its power. In the next 20 minutes, all networks will be flooded with its virus.'

You will read a lot of advice about **dialogue tags**. These are verbs or adverbs used to describe how something is spoken, such as *whispered, panted, hissed, hastily, angrily* or *softly*. If you do use dialogue tags other than *said*, use them sparingly to create **mood** and **character**.

Activity 2

Match the **dialogue tag** to its dialogue. Each tag can only be used once.

a 'It is NOT the end of the world!'	**i** she panted.
b 'Over here!'	**ii** he shouted.
c 'Why would anyone trust you?'	**iii** he stated with confidence.
d 'We need to go through that forest and somehow across the river on the other side.'	**iv** she queried.
e 'I can't. Go. On.'	**v** I exclaimed.
f 'I did it!'	**vi** Martha called.
g 'Is it dead?'	**vii** June sneered.
h 'There's no way we can make it to the cemetery before midnight. We're doomed.'	**viii** he cried.

Language feature

Vocabulary

It's important that you use **vocabulary** relevant to the story **genre** you are writing.

Activity 3

Here is a list of words appropriate to use in your horror story to describe **settings**, **characters** and **feelings**. Write a **definition** for each word, using a dictionary when needed.

unearthly

menacing

suspense

dread

horrendous

wraith

wretched

phantom

ghoul

ominous

Activity 4

Choose five of the words from the activity above and use each one in a separate sentence below. Remember to try to write sentences appropriate to a **horror story**!

a ____________________

____

b ____________________

____

c ____________________

____

d ____________________

____

e ____________________

____

Language feature

Onomatopoeia

Onomatopoeic words try to **capture sounds** such as *rattle*, *squeal* or *hiss*. These words are useful to create atmosphere. Using sounds that evoke feelings of fear and curiosity can increase tension in horror stories.

Activity 5

Match the **onomatopoeic word** to its appropriate object or place.

a	moan	wind
b	swoosh	high heels
c	bang	child
d	clang	door
e	creak	ghoul
f	rustle	gate
g	snarl	beast
h	whimper	chair
i	hiss	ghost
j	boo	cat
k	clack	leaves

Language feature

Symbolism

Genre stories often use easily identifiable **symbols** that **signal specific ideas**. For example, in fantasy stories gemstones have secret powers and in horror stories a full moon is a symbol that something bad will happen.

You can read more about symbolism on page 92.

Activity 6

Match each **symbol** to its meaning.

a	dove	**i**	disease and pestilence
b	cross	**ii**	peace
c	skull	**iii**	bad news is coming
d	mirror	**iv**	death
e	sun	**v**	love and romance
f	crow	**vi**	faith in God
g	storm	**vii**	happiness
h	rat	**viii**	bad omen
i	rose	**ix**	truth and honesty

Activity 7

Write three **symbols** you might find or use in a **horror story**. For each one, explain what **idea or emotion** it represents.

a ______________________________

____

b ______________________________

____

c ______________________________

____

Spotlight *on spelling*

Turning nouns into adjectives

Short stories are brought to life by the use of evocative **descriptions**. The most common way to add description is to use **adjectives**.

Many adjectives are made from nouns by adding the suffix *y*. For most words, you simply add the suffix *y* to the base word.
swamp + *y* → swamp**y**

For words ending in a consonant, vowel and then a consonant you must double the consonant and then add *y* to the base word.
bag + *y* → ba**gy**

For words ending in *e*, drop the *e* and add *y* to the base word.
ice + *y* → ic**y**

Activity 1

Identify the spelling errors in the sentences below.

Write the correct **spelling** of each incorrect word on the line provided.

a The little girl stood with her skinney arm outstretched. ______________

b The bubbling bog was smelley and unpleasant. ______________

c We prayed for a sunney day. ______________

d My blankets were lumppy and uncomfortable. ______________

e The road was bumppy and made me feel afraid. ______________

f She has a light, breezzy manner that did not convey the truth of her troubled mind. ______________

g We opened the door to discover a messey and abandoned room. ______________

h I picked the bright red berry and bit into its tastey flesh. ______________

i We knew that visiting the cemetery at night would be scarry. ______________

Below is a list of more **suffixes** used to change nouns into **adjectives**. Note that with some suffixes you will need to change the base word.

beauty + *ful* → beautiful

joy + *ous* → joyous

anxiety + *ious* → anxious

base + *ic* → basic

identity + *ical* → identical

Activity 2

Change the nouns below to **adjectives** using the given **suffix**.

a monster + *ous* ______________

b space + *ious* ______________

c myth + *ical* ______________

d caution + *ous* ______________

e hysteria + *ical* ______________

f acrobat + *ic* ______________

g delicacy + *ious* ______________

You be the teacher

Below is a **complication paragraph** for a horror story written by a Year 10 student. There are some errors in the structure of the paragraph and the spelling of some of the words. Can you correct the mistakes? Rewrite the paragraph with the **correct structure** and with the **correct spelling of all words**.

Taking a deep breath of cold air, I pushed open the creakey door and disappeared into the gloomey darkness. An icey wind was blowing, and I rubbed my acheing frozen fingers under my armpits. Clouds started covering the moon as I arrived at the terrible place where John was being held captive. Standing in front of the imposing wooden door, I dared not try to imagine what lay beyond.

Now you write

It is now time for you to complete your own **horror story**.

1. Before you write, take some time to look at the student writing sample on the following page as a guide to writing standards.
2. Once you have read the student writing sample, take some time to think about what you believe are the most important features of a horror story that you need to master. Use the space below to jot down your answer to this question:
   What do you find most difficult when writing this kind of text?
3. Now look at the imaginative text marking criteria on page viii to double-check that you understand the requirements for a really good piece of imaginative writing.
   Remember that you have already done your planning and drafted your orientation, complication paragraphs and resolution. Use your own paper. Good luck!

Looking at other students' writing

Genre short stories:
Write a horror story about a deserted house.

Orientattion
A strong orientation grabs hold of and intrigues the reader, and sets up expectations of what is to come.

Narrative techniques
Descriptive language engages the reader's imagination. Tension is built effectively through a slow build-up from everyday events to strange happenings.

Text structure
The short story is well structured, featuring an obvious orientation, complication and resolution.

Paragraphing
A new paragraph is used to introduce each main part of the story's action.

ADVANCED SAMPLE

WRITE A HORROR STORY ABOUT A DESERTED HOUSE.

The rain hammered ceaselessly on the windowpanes, leaving the glass scarred with crooked streams of water. Jane struggled to see the yard beyond, barely making out the dull yellow of the old groundskeeper's cottage. The weather had been awful for the last week, trapping Jane indoors, something she resented. There was nothing to do in her grandmother's house. No television, no computers, not even a radio.

As she flicked her eyes back to the gloom outside the window, a dark figure caught her eye. It was perhaps no bigger than a child, and seemed to scurry from behind the furthest hedge and disappear behind the groundskeeper's cottage. The cottage, just like her grandmother's house, was empty. A slight shiver fingered its way up Jane's spine. Logic told her it would simply be an animal of sorts—a stray dog or an overfed possum. Her irrational side spoke more loudly, however, and prompted her to head to the front door. Without a thought about the icy rain or the growling thunder, Jane rushed into the yard.

The run from the house to the cottage left Jane soaked through and heaving heavy breaths. With a great effort, she hushed her breathing, trying her best not to reveal her presence to whatever the thing was that had entered the cottage before her. She crouched low to the ground and shuffled along until she was squatting underneath the main window of the small building. Having played here many times in her childhood, it was not unfamiliar, yet something told her to be cautious. Raising herself onto her tiptoes, Jane braved a peep into the window. What she saw was shocking.

Bent awkwardly over the small stove was a pale-faced creature. It had long thin limbs, bent at odd angles, and an impossibly small torso. Jane involuntarily let out an audible gasp, and quickly reached up to cover her mouth. What was that thing? Was she dreaming? Such things should not exist. As she continued watching, she saw that the strange creature appeared to be cooking something in a small iron pot. It occurred to Jane right then that she must act now, whilst it was occupied. Looking around her for a weapon, her eyes fell upon a rusty shovel. Perfect. Picking it up without a sound, Jane armed herself for a fight.

Jane stood up to her full height and held the shovel out in front of her. She walked the short distance to the cottage door and, without a pause, kicked it hard. She charged into the room and her shovel crashed down heavily onto something hard in front of her, bringing with it two loud screams. Opening her eyes, Jane was startled to see the face of the creature. It was not horrid or ghastly. Rather, it was terrified, yet gentle. It was the face of the groundskeeper she had known and loved for years, only he was much, much older. Standing with quivering hands, looking at the broken chair she had attacked, Jane felt very foolish indeed. How had she forgotten that Groundskeeper Joe was still alive?

Vocabulary
Complex vocabulary is used. A variety of strong adjectives and verbs enhances the images created, e.g. *scurry, fingered, audible, scarred.*

Sentence structure
A variety of sentence lengths is used to avoid monotony and create interest. Short sentences create drama. Phrases and fragments are used to good narrative effect, e.g. *no television, no computers, not even a radio.*

Ideas
The horror story theme (the empty house) is developed and sustained throughout.

Spelling
All words are spelt correctly, including some difficult or challenging words, e.g. *involuntarily, audible, irrational.*

Punctuation
Correct punctuation is used, with commas cleverly placed in complex sentences.

Cohesion
There is continuity of ideas throughout the description—the focus is always on Jane's experience in the house.

UNIT TWELVE

Imaginative texts
Journal entries

Understanding the question

Imagine you are a scientist. Write a journal entry reflecting on the day you made an important discovery.

Type of question

This question is asking you to write a particular type of imaginative text—a **journal entry**.

A journal is a **personal reflection on a recent event**. The purpose of a journal entry is to give the reader a vivid image of a particular event. A journal entry will focus on a few main elements of a person's day, and reflect on their thoughts and feelings about that event. Journal entries are often factual, however for this task we are focusing on writing an imaginative journal entry.

You are being asked to write an imaginative journal entry, where you take on the persona of a scientist.

Features of a journal entry

- Aims to recount an event or experience, focusing on the writer's feelings
- Concentrates on key incidents or moments and does not include every single detail of a day
- Uses temporal connectives to show the connections between events
- Is written as a series of chronological paragraphs, providing a sense of time and sequence, in first-person narrative
- Is usually informal and personal language which can be emotive
- Begins with the date at the top of the page
- Includes a range of sentence lengths

1 Use a dictionary to define the words below.

a scientist

____

____

b journal

____

____

c reflecting

____

____

d discovery

____

____

2 Below are six different fields that scientists work in and two different discoveries relevant to each field—one made and one yet to be made. Match the discoveries to the correct scientific field.

a Neuroscience	**i** the impact sun spots have on Earth
	ii the origins of dreams
b Astronomy	**iii** how plants communicate
	iv why bees collect pollen
c Meteorology	**v** how to tell the gender of plants
	vi what causes tsunamis
d Zoology	**vii** why our heartbeat changes
	viii how memory works
e Botany	**ix** the cure for cancer
	x the relationship between the tide and the moon
f Biology	**xi** why cats purr
	xii why the polar icecaps are melting

3 Look at the list of scientific fields above. Which fields of science do you find the most interesting? Write down the two you would most like to learn more about.

____

____

Planning and organisation

TIP Do some research about the person whose perspective you are trying to capture—a scientist. Find out about their life and what their main scientific discoveries have been. This will ensure you effectively capture the voice of the person and create a realistic portrait of their world.

Even though you might know a lot about your topic—the scientist and their discoveries—it's still really important to **plan**! If you don't know a lot about a specific scientist or discovery, you may need to do a bit of **research**. Below is an example of the type of information you will need to help you plan your journal entry.

Name: Galileo Galilei

Lived: Pisa, Italy (1564–1642)

Brief description of his world:

* time of the Roman Inquisition, when the Roman Catholic Church investigated and punished people whose ideas conflicted with those of the church
* beginnings of the scientific revolution, which saw people begin to develop scientific theories about the natural world.

Significant discoveries:

* constructed an improved telescope: Galileo improved the magnification of the telescopic lens so he could see further and more clearly. With his telescope he discovered the four satellites of Jupiter.
* supported the theory of Heliocentrism which claimed that the sun is at the centre of our solar system. This theory was considered false and contrary to scripture during Galileo's lifetime, however this theory was later proven correct.

1 Choose one of Galileo's discoveries from the list above and **brainstorm** how the day of his discovery might have unfolded. This can be a series of dot points or a couple of sentences.

You might want to include reference to any or all of the following:

- what time of day he woke up
- what he ate
- what the weather was like
- where he was working
- who he spoke with
- what emotions he was feeling during the day.

Remember that this is an **imaginative** writing task, so not all of your content needs to be entirely factual. Be creative with your ideas.

2 Name three scientists who have made remarkable scientific discoveries. Beside each name, briefly describe what they discovered.

3 Choose one of the scientists from the question above to further research their life and world as a basis for your writing task. Complete the table below.

Note: if you like, you could write your journal entry about one of Galileo's discoveries and use the information provided on page 121.

Name	
Lived/Lives	
Brief description of their world	
Significant discovery	

Structure

The **journal entry** you are going to write will be a personal recount of a memorable event. This means that it is likely to be **structured chronologically**, which means the events will be recounted in the order in which they happened.

Opening paragraph

At the top of the **opening paragraph**, you must include the **date** that the journal entry was written. Make sure you put a date that is contextually correct for your chosen scientist's discovery. For example, a journal entry written by Charles Darwin about his discovery of the theory of evolution would be dated some time in 1859.

The opening paragraph will typically **begin with a general sentence about the day**, e.g. *Today was a memorable day!* The opening paragraph will then present a **brief overview of how the writer is feeling**. For example, *It is quite remarkable and I can't quite believe it, but I think today I may have finally discovered how the tide is controlled by the moon!*

Activity 1

Write an **opening sentence** to express the following feelings and emotions about a scientific work or discovery.

a disappointed ____________________

____

____

b excited ____________________

____

____

c frustrated ____________________

____

____

d surprised ____________________

____

____

e pleased ____________________

____

____

Activity 2

Write the **opening paragraph** for your **journal entry** about a scientific discovery. Use your own paper.

Body paragraphs

This is a series of **related paragraphs** that describe, in detail, **what happened** during the day, **how the writer felt** about these experiences and **how this will affect their future**. For the scientific discovery topic, you will be describing the nature of the discovery and how the scientist feels about it.

The following example body paragraph is from an imaginary journal entry by Sir Isaac Newton:

> The exact nature of my discovery is rather interesting, some might say amusing. I had been working in my study since before the sun peeped over the mountains. It must have been near 5 am when my restless mind drew me from my sleeping chamber. I read for some time by the light of my flickering candle and then tried fruitlessly to write. Frustration took me outside around mid-morning and I found myself enjoying the autumn air that swirled through the leaves of the apple tree under which I was sitting. Then it hit me! An apple—right on my head!

Activity 3

a Underline all the references in the paragraph above to the world in which Newton lived.

b Circle all of the references to **time**.

c Highlight any words or phrases that express how Newton is **feeling**.

Activity 4

Here are a student's notes for the **body paragraphs** for a journal entry written from the perspective of Benjamin Franklin. It is about the day he discovered that lightning is electrical. Put the notes in chronological order.

______ His son assisted him in raising the kite.

______ He didn't tell anyone except his son about his planned experiment.

______ He prepared a large silk handkerchief and two cross-sticks as a makeshift kite.

______ He decided to test his theory that lightning is electrical.

______ He had the idea to add a key to the tail of the kite.

______ He walked into the fields and set up watch in a shed, waiting for the coming storm.

______ Lightning struck the kite and he collected 'electric fire'.

Activity 5

Draft a **body paragraph** for your **journal entry** about a scientific discovery.

Concluding paragraph

The **concluding paragraph** is a **final comment about how the person is feeling** once the moment has been recounted.

For example: What a marvellous and unbelievable thing it seems now that it is written down!

A journal entry usually ends with a focus on what will come the next day.

For example: I'm eager to find out what tomorrow will bring. The weather promises to be even more stormy!

Activity 6

Draft the **concluding paragraph** for your journal entry about the scientific discovery. Use your own paper for this activity.

Language feature

TIP If you are writing from the perspective of an actual scientist, it might help to find some writing by that person. Reading this will give you a sense of their voice, and help when you write your journal entry.

Expressing feelings

When writing a journal entry, you must try to **capture the emotions** of the writer. These feelings are typically expressed by **syntax**, **punctuation** and **word choice**.

There are many different words that may describe a scientist's feelings.

For example: grumpy, critical, frustrated, optimistic, eager, hurt, joyous, depressed, enthusiastic

Activity 1

Below is a list of sentences, each expressing a specific **feeling** which is written in brackets. For each sentence, briefly explain how the feeling is expressed to the reader. Focus on **word choice**, **punctuation** and **syntax**.

Syntax is the way in which words are arranged in a sentence.

The first one has been done for you.

a It's over—the experiment has failed and I do not wish to continue! (grumpy)

The use of the exclamation mark shows that the writer is passionate about what they are saying. Also the negative connotations of the words *failed* and *do not wish* show that the writer is unhappy.

b He didn't even bother to read my most recent letter. I saw it unopened on his desk. I don't know that I will survive rejection again. (hurt)

____

c Of course, the weather decided to change just as I was about to test my latest theory. It feels like my chance will never come! (disappointed)

____

d The Inquisition is reading his latest publication. Well, they say they are, but I doubt they would even understand what they're reading! (bitter)

____

Activity 2

Each sentence below captures a particular type of **feeling**. Rewrite each sentence to reflect a **different** feeling but keep the basic content the same. You can change or add words as needed.

a confident: *This will certainly mean the beginning of my career as a successful scientist!*

anxious: ______________________________

b inspired: *The beauty of atoms is in their dynamic and unexpected behaviour which continues to cause me both surprise and excitement about what their interactions mean.*

confused: ______________________________

c frustrated: *Once again the weather had foiled my plans to view the lunar eclipse.*

excited: ______________________________

d unsure: *The size of the patient's heart seemed to be far larger than is normal and I did not know what dissection would reveal.*

enthusiastic: ______________________________

e defeated: *I decided by lunchtime that my experiment would not work and that I had been crazy to think it ever could be possible to understand the true cause of dreams.*

optimistic: ______________________________

Language feature

Imagery

The type of **journal writing** you are being asked to do for this question is **imaginative**. Consequently, you must use your imagination to add engaging and interesting details to your recount of a memorable event. You must also try to capture the world of your chosen persona and their feelings through your writing.

One very effective way of making a piece of writing engaging is to use **imagery**. Imagery is the **creation of mental pictures using figures of speech** such as similes, metaphors and personification.

A **simile** is a comparison between two things using the words *like* or *as*.
For example: I was as happy as a sunflower in spring.

A **metaphor** is a direct comparison between two things.
For example: I was drowning in a sea of ideas.

Personification is giving human characteristics to non-human objects.
For example: The electricity danced through his veins and I could see his eyes flutter open.

Activity 3

Write the **figure of speech** being used in each example on the lines below.

a The radiant golden orb peeped over the lush green hills. ____________________

b The blank page haunted me in my sleep. ____________________

c The document loaded as slowly as my grandma crosses the road. ____________________

d My son was a gentle lamb, asleep in his cot. ____________________

e At my feet my elderly Labrador snored like an old man. ______

f Through my window I could see the frenzied dance of the trees and the driving rain pounding the fragile daffodils that dotted our garden. ______

g At 10 am my darling husband entered the room, bringing with him a breakfast as wholesome as a sun shower. ______

h I will never outshine him. His theories replicate more quickly than rabbits.
______

i All down the page the pen's black blood dripped, smearing my precious words and obscuring my findings. ______

Activity 4

You have been given a list of objects. Write a sentence describing each object through the use of a **figure of speech** (simile, metaphor, personification). Try to capture the quality given in brackets. The first one has been done for you.

a The moon through the window (its size and colour) Through my half-open shutters I spied the moon, a giant golden ball sparkling in the darkness.

b The light of a lamp (its brightness) ______

c A broken computer (its noise) ______

d A leaking pen (the colour of the ink) ______

e A cup of tea (its heat) ______

Activity 5

Use a **figure of speech** (simile, metaphor, personification) to create an image of the given objects, places or people below.

a A scientist ______

b A hopeless assistant ______

c The early morning sun rising ______

d Feeling tired ______

Spotlight *on spelling*

Adding the suffixes *ful* and *fully*

When writing an **imaginative journal entry**, you will need to use a range of **adverbs** and **adjectives** to describe the emotions and experiences of your persona. To turn a noun into an adjective or adverb, you sometimes need to add the suffixes *ful* or *fully*. Below are the rules for adding these suffixes.

The suffix ***ful*** only has one *l*, not two. For most words, to make the adjective, just add the suffix *ful* to the base word without making any changes. To make the adverb, add ***fully*** (*ful* + *ly*). Never drop the final *e* and don't double any letters at the end of a word.

For example:

success + *ful*	→	success**ful**	+ *fully*	→ success**fully**
dread + *ful*	→	dread**ful**	+ *fully*	→ dread**fully**
care + *ful*	→	care**ful**	+ *fully*	→ care**fully**

However, base words ending in *y* need to drop the *y* and add *i* before adding the suffix *ful* or *fully*.

For example:

mercy + *ful*	→	merci**ful**	+ *fully*	→ merci**fully**
beauty + *ful*	→	beauti**ful**	+ *fully*	→ beauti**fully**

Activity 1

Add the suffixes *ful* and *fully* to the words below.

a cheer ____________________ ____________________

b care ____________________ ____________________

c deceit ____________________ ____________________

d dread ____________________ ____________________

e plenty ____________________ ____________________

f force ____________________ ____________________

g fright ____________________ ____________________

Activity 2

Circle the correct spelling of the word in brackets.

a The students behaved (disgracefully/disgracfully) on camp.

b Mary was very (boastful/boasttful) about her success in the finals.

c My mother says my dreams to be an actor are (fancyfull/fanciful).

d The paramedics were incredibly (helpfull/helpful) the day my mother was ill.

e We must treat the prisoners as (mercyfully/mercifully) as we can.

f Our puppy Miena looked up at me (pitifully/pityfully) when she saw me filling the dog bath.

g I must (regretfully/regrettfully) inform you that your application was not successful.

h Heather danced (beautyfully/beautifully) across the stage.

You be the teacher

Below is a **body paragraph** for a journal entry written by a Year 10 student. There are some errors in the structure of the paragraph and the spelling of some words. Can you correct the mistakes? Rewrite the paragraph with the **correct structure** and with the **correct spelling of all words**.

Could this be the evidence that Venus has an atmosphere? By 8 pm, the weather was perfect for searching the sky with my telescope. The new lens is much more powerfull than my first one! There she was! Looking deeply and carfully into the lens, I discerned that the planet had indeed moved. At this point my heart began to race quite rapidly. I had my telescope directed to where I knew Venus—my wonderful planet of love—resided.

Now you write

It is now time for you to complete your own **journal entry** about a scientific discovery.

1. Before you write, take some time to look at the student writing sample on the following page as a guide to writing standards.

2. Once you have read the student writing sample, take some time to think about what you believe are the most important features of a journal entry that you need to master. Use the space below to jot down your answer to this question:
What do you find most difficult when writing this kind of text?

3. Now look at the imaginative text marking criteria on page viii to double-check that you understand the requirements for a really good piece of imaginative writing.
Remember that you have already done your planning and drafted your opening paragraph, one body paragraph and concluding paragraph. Use your own paper. Good luck!

Looking at other students' writing

Imagine you are a young artist in Paris in the 1930s.
Write a journal about the day you first saw a Picasso painting.

Orientation
The strong orientation grabs the reader's attention through the use of an engaging personal voice and description.

Narrative techniques
Descriptive language engages the reader's imagination. Humour and emotive language are used well.

Text structure
The journal entry is well structured, featuring an obvious opening, orientating the reader, and a concluding paragraph thinking about the future.

Paragraphing
A new paragraph is used to introduce each new element of the day's events being recounted.

ADVANCED SAMPLE

IMAGINE YOU ARE A YOUNG ARTIST IN PARIS IN THE 1930S. WRITE A JOURNAL ABOUT THE DAY YOU FIRST SAW A PICASSO PAINTING APRIL 1938.

Dear Diary,

What a wonderfully surprising and inspiring day! It started lazily, as I woke after noon, hot and sticky from having overslept in the early summer heat. My breakfast was basic—black coffee and a croissant from a little place around the corner. The grubby boy who served me very nearly put me off my food, but it was cheap and all I needed to fuel me through the day.

I decided not to go into the afternoon art class. I know tomorrow that my instructor will be unimpressed, and likely ensure that I have the most appalling pallete to work with, but what I saw today makes all of tomorrow's hardships worth it. Whilst at the café ordering my breakfast, I overheard a couple whispering enthusiastically about a new work of art that they had just seen. It was a new Picasso.

Now Picasso is a name I have heard many, many times. I have seen perhaps three or four reproductions of his work—sketches of his paintings made hastily by mediocre artists, hoping to make a dollar from Picasso's talent. But to see an original! Well, the prospect was too good for me to waste, and so I scribbled the name of the gallery on the greasy paper bag from my croissant, and headed out into the sunshine. I can't even really explain how I felt. My insides squirmed with a mixture of anticipation and nerves.

The gallery itself was tiny, no more than the size of a dining room but without the table and chairs. The poorly plastered walls were covered with perhaps 10 or 15 paintings of various sizes. I pushed through a small group of well-dressed young men, heading towards the far end of the room.

I'm not sure what overwhelmed me first—the colours or the figure. Both were astounding. Central to the image was the face of a woman, weeping. The lower half of her face was pale—drained of colour as asymmetrical tears flooded her cheeks. Juxtaposed to this were the bold reds, greens and yellows of her hair and hat. It was like her sorrow had leaked down her face, and the colours of life were mocking her. This was like no portrait I had ever seen. There was no explaining the lines of the image and how Picasso had captured the suffering of the woman. My heart ached to think of her grief-widened eyes.

Now that I am home and reflecting on this experience, I feel both spurred on to paint in challenging and new ways, but also overwhelmed and intimidated. Perhaps my work will never rival that of such a great artist and, if it will not, is it worth painting at all? I suppose tomorrow will determine my fate, as I will seek my muse.

Vocabulary
Complex vocabulary is used throughout. A variety of adjectives and strong verbs are used to enhance the images created, e.g. *scribbled, squirmed, greasy.*

Sentence structure
A variety of sentence lengths is used to avoid monotony and create interest. Short sentences create drama.

Ideas
The focus of the journal entry (seeing the Picasso painting) is developed and sustained throughout.

Cohesion
There is continuity of ideas throughout the journal entry. Focus is always on the main event of the day: seeing the painting.

Punctuation
Correct punctuation is used. Complex punctuation is used where required.

Spelling
All words are spelt correctly. There is frequent inclusion of correctly spelt difficult or challenging words, e.g. *asymmetrical, juxtaposed* and *overwhelmed.*

Selected answers

UNIT 1 Argument essays

Understanding the question page 1

1 (suggested answers)
- a what time to be home on weeknights
- b how many hours teenagers spend online
- c when they get their first car

2 (suggested answers)
- a who to date
- b who to be friends with
- c what university to attend
- d what to wear

Planning and organisation page 2

1 FOR (suggested answers): the decisions personally affect the teenagers, they know more about a situation, they are developing their autonomy
AGAINST (suggested answers): too young to make big decisions, easily influenced by peers, adolescent brain not fully developed, influenced by media

Structure pages 3–5

1
- a *Relevant background information:* the world is rapidly changing, many technological innovations in the last 100 years
  Definition of key terms: dependence—people feel the need to rely on it for support, or even survival.
  Writer's thesis: People today are becoming increasingly more dependent on technology, with potentially serious consequences.
  Three main arguments: People are becoming overly reliant on digital entertainment, mobile phones and domestic appliances.
- b Are people too dependent on technology?

3
- a *Statement*: Mobile phones are one piece of technology that people are definitely addicted to.
- b *Evidence*: According to FoneBank Australia, over 88% of Australians own a mobile phone. Mobile phones are now so technologically advanced that they allow people to access the internet, listen to music, use GPS, take video and pictures, play video games and even monitor their own heart rate.
- c *Why*: Mobile phones are definitely one form of technology that people are far too dependent on.

Language feature pages 6–7

1
- a People today are too obsessed with technology.
- b The death penalty is never acceptable.
- c Many families use a lot of technology.

2
- b Some families speak highly of the impact of technology on learning.
- c Take this opportunity to be heard.
- d The closing of the bridge will affect some people's ability to arrive at work on time.
- e Nothing is quite as devastating as the loss of a pet dog.
- f People must respect one another, regardless of gender or race.

3 American filmmaker Spike Jonze is one of the most creative and innovative directors of the 21st century. His films focus on subcultures and the human psyche and inspire people to think in new ways about society and themselves. Jonze's films are a portal into secret worlds.

Spotlight on spelling pages 8–9

1
- a disjoint
- b disempower
- c deconstruct
- d devalue
- e illogical
- f inappropriate
- g incapable
- h irresponsible

2
- a irregular
- b impossible
- c immobil
- d disembody
- e unhappy
- f unnatural

3
- a impossible
- b deconstruction
- c empower
- d devaluing
- e inappropriate
- f unhappy

You be the teacher page 9

Decisions are difficult to make, yet sometimes this difficulty must be endured by teenagers alone. It is impossible for parents to know everything about teenagers' lives, because teenagers often have secrets that are too embarrassing or personal to share with their parents. Secrets should be respected, as long as they do not relate to illegal or irresponsible activities. Consequently, parents are unable to make decisions relating to secrets, therefore teenagers must be allowed to make decisions for themselves.

Understanding the question page 12

1 view or judgement formed about something, not necessarily based on fact or knowledge

3 Possible answers include natural resources, censorship, education, terrorism and racism.

Planning and organisation pages 13–14

1 (suggested answers) *Definition of climate change*: the long-term changes to the Earth's climate
Reasons why people believe in climate change: Scientific evidence shows that the Earth's climate has changed throughout history. However, over the last 1300 years, the rate of warming of the Earth's temperature has increased rapidly. People believe this is a direct result of human activities, especially the burning of fossil fuels.
Reasons why people don't believe in climate change: Some evidence exists that Arctic ice has increased by 50% since 2012; unreliability of climate change models used by scientists exaggerate the problem; no direct evidence that the current trend in warming is caused by man.

Structure pages 14–17

1
- **a** genetically modified food
- **b** negative
- **c** that genetically modified foods will save mankind

2 The pop music industry is problematic.

4
- **a** the effectiveness of science
- **b** The writer wishes for the readers to appreciate the contributions that science has made to mankind.
- **c** I am not sure how one would estimate the number of lives this achievement has saved over the past century and a half, but it's almost certainly in the hundreds of millions.
- **d** ...the modern Western lifespan has increased by 20 or so years since the industrial revolution through the scientific discovery of germ theory...

5 Example one is the most effective introduction for an opinion piece because it shows strong feelings and appropriate content; for example, 'But the best-case scenario from a climate perspective would be if all seven billion of us woke up one day and realised that the vegans were right all along.'

Language feature pages 18–19

1
- **a** People have no interest in sustainability as it might negatively impact their lifestyles.
- **b** The earth is warming at alarming rates yet no one is doing anything.
- **c** Parents must work at becoming healthier so they will be more active for their children.
- **d** The number of female coders is dropping while the demand for coders is soaring.
- **e** Children enjoy playing outside because they love playing in the open.
- **f** Volunteering is easy and many people do it regularly.

2 (suggested answers)
- **a** Are they a showcase for new possibilities?
- **b** I am a master mapmaker!
- **c** You must complete all five of the game's missions.
- **d** Did we win?
- **e** You must support our project.
- **f** Do you love the idea?

3
- **a** statement
- **b** exclamation
- **c** statement
- **d** command
- **e** question
- **f** exclamation
- **g** exclamation
- **h** question

Spotlight on spelling pages 20–21

1
- **a** object: to show disapproval or disagreement with something
  object: something that can be seen and touched
- **b** produce: a collection of agricultural or natural products
  produce: to make something from raw materials
- **c** minute: one-sixtieth of an hour
  minute: a very small measure or amount
- **d** frequent: happening often over short intervals
  frequent: to visit somewhere often
- **e** desert: a dry environment due to very little rainfall
  desert: to abandon a group, individual or place
- **f** entrance: to be put into a trance
  entrance: the opening to a place
- **g** moped: past tense of the word *mope*, which means 'to sulk or be visibly unhappy'
  moped: a low-powered motorised vehicle with two wheels

2
- **a** insight: penetrating mental vision
  incite: to encourage one to action
- **b** cite: to quote, usually from an authority
  sight: the power of seeing
- **c** taut: pulled tightly
  taught: past tense of the verb teach
- **d** manner: a way of doing something
  manor: the mansion and land belonging to a lord

3
- **a** presence
- **b** principle
- **c** course
- **d** intense
- **e** guessed
- **f** piece
- **g** allowed

You be the teacher page 22

I truly believe that all cars should be banned. In Australia the number of passenger vehicles per 1000 people has increased from 153 in 1955 to 695 today. The death of *all* passenger vehicles would be the lifeline our world desperately needs. It's a fact that cars are killing the planet. They really are. Those loud, smelly metallic monsters eat up our land and eat up the ozone layer. It's disgusting. Our country's obsession with cars has got to end, or else we will find ourselves living in a land of tar and fog.

UNIT 3 Television advertisement scripts

Understanding the question page 24

1 script (noun): the written text of a play of film
script (verb): the act of writing the text for a play or film

Structure pages 26–29

1 **i** **a** muesli **b** luscious, plum, crunchy, crisp
ii **a** pop songs compilation
b All the pop songs you love to sing along to

2 **a** chocolate bar **b** shampoo
c sports car **d** mobile phone plan
e car insurance

4 (suggested answers)
a Celebrity endorsement because people associate being beautiful with celebrities. Also, many celebrities endorse perfumes.
b Testimonials from everyday people because dishwashing is a job of the everyday person, so we would trust them more.
c Guilt because parents want their children to be healthy and feel guilty if they don't do everything they can to achieve this.
d Appeal to vanity because moisturiser is designed to make skin look more beautiful.

5 **a** girl on her phone
b a man brushing his teeth
c dog catching a frisbee
d children playing in a front yard

6 **a** A hint of jasmine, a touch of jonquil, a mix of lavender.
There's nothing purer than the smell of fresh flowers.
Make a statement.
Wear *Flowers* by Renata.
b (Suggested answer) A close-up of flowers blowing in the breeze. Zoom out to show a woman standing in a field of flowers, looking beautiful and holding a bottle of *Flowers*.

Language features pages 30–32

1 **b** hair gel **c** school shoes
d digital watch **e** laptop

2 (suggested answers)
b Twice the chocolate and three times the caramel of other chocolate bars.
c No other chip has this much crunch.
d Made by nature, not scientists.

3 (suggested answers)
b What do you get from a pampered cow? Spoiled milk.
This is funny because the homograph *spoiled* means both food that is off and also being pampered.
c When a clock is hungry it goes back four seconds.
This is funny because the word *four* is a homophone for *for*. Here the word *four* refers to both time and going back for a second helping of food.
d When she told me I was average, she was just being mean.
This is funny because the word *mean* is a homograph and refers to both the behaviour of being cruel and the mathematical term meaning 'average'.
e I used to hate maths but then I realised decimals have a point.
This is funny because the phrase *have a point* refers to both having a purpose and the point in a decimal number.

4 (suggested answers)
a sole/soul (a shoe shop)
Our shoes are good for your soul.
b roar/raw (sushi restaurant)
Sushi Niro will give you something to roar about.
c flaw/floor (flooring company)
Our flooring is flawless.
d use/ewes (knitted jumper)
We only ewes the best wool for your winter sweaters.

Spotlight on spelling pages 32–33

1 **a** S **b** H **c** S **d** S **e** S **f** S **g** H **h** H
2 **a** H **b** H **c** H **d** H **e** S **f** S **g** S **h** S

You be the teacher page 33

Sun, surf and fitness! A mid-week event, the Manly-to-the-Spit short race attracts up to 3000 people annually. The course is only 8 km, making it perfect for the entire family. Register now to get the discounted early-bird rates and celebrate summer with a bit of healthy competition.

UNIT 4

Proposals

Understanding the question page 35

1 offer, suggest, recommend

2 **a** new and creative
b a means to solving a problem
c being untidy with rubbish
d performed in open view of others

Structure pages 38–41

1 **a** Skateboard riders do not have enough safe, purposely designated spaces to ride in our council area. As a result, skaters are often riding in public spaces, including roads, and being seen as a nuisance by the general public.
b Without a designated space, skaters are at risk of being hit by cars or involved in disputes with non-skaters.
c There are many underutilised public spaces, such as under bridges, that could be easily converted into skate bowls to accommodate the needs of skaters. Such an innovative solution has had great success in other suburban areas, including suburbs in Brisbane and Melbourne.

2 2, 1, 3

4 Young people from the age of 16 should be given the opportunity to vote before the 2020 election. This will give them a voice in the major decisions affecting the future of their country.

7 (suggested answers)
a Promote healthy eating through television advertisements and presentations at schools.
b Introduce confessional booths into the school where students can share, confidentially, their experiences of bullying.
c Drop leaflets to all homes within the region and hold a rally outside the council chambers in August.
d Introduce paid trolleys by the end of June and promote this through signs around the car park.

9 **a** Increased number of desexed cats and decreased number of unwanted kittens
b Decreased number of feral cats in Lane Cove National Park
c The health and safety of our native fauna is at risk if we do not act now and implement this proposed solution to the growing feral cat population in Lane Cove National Park.

Language features pages 41–42

1 **a** iii **b** i **c** iv **d** ii

2 **a** i **b** i **c** i

Spotlight on spelling pages 42–43

1 **a** foreign **b** reign **c** receipt **d** leisure **e** weird
f friend **g** achieve **h** veil
i ceiling **j** neighbour **k** seize

2 Neighbourhood, achieve, Friends, their, neighbours, forfeit.

You be the teacher pages 43–44

Correct structure:

Our primary objective is to decrease the weekly incidence of cyberbullying in our school by the end of the year. Our main strategy to achieve this goal is to raise awareness of the positive benefits of spending more time away from screens. The number one activity we plan to implement to support this strategy is the introduction of an afterschool fun club once a week. This club will help students discover their creativity and encourage them to pursue non-digital activities in their spare time. We firmly believe that this will lead to a decrease in cyberbullying at our school. It is important that we act now to address the negative impact that cyberbullying is having on children in primary school.

UNIT 5

Critical analysis essays

Understanding the question page 46

2 **a** the state of being where a child is naïve and ignorant in respect to the sometimes complex and difficult world of adulthood
b to share or exchange information

Planning and organisation pages 47–49

1 **a** 1757–1827 **b** Mainly London, England
c 'London'
d Romantic—Blake started writing poetry celebrating nature, but ended up writing poetry critical of the industrial world and London.
e Poetry, painting, print-making and his contribution to the Romantic movement

3 **a** The speaker (presumably a young chimney sweep) and Tom Dacre
b A young boy telling of how he became a chimney sweeper: his mother died when he was a very small child and he was sold by his father to a person who trades in young chimney sweepers. He describes a boy, younger than the speaker, called Tom Dacre who is scared and sad about joining the chimney sweepers. The speaker comforts Tom and tells him having a shaved head means the soot from the chimneys won't ruin his white hair. Tom dreams that night of all the little chimney sweepers being locked in coffins, and an angel freeing them. This reassures Tom, and he wakes in the morning happy to go off and do his job as a chimney sweeper. This poem is a critique of the adults

who treat children so poorly, suggesting that faith in God is their only hope for happiness.

4
- a 'weep, 'weep
- b This sound imagery reveals to the reader how small the child was when he was first made a chimney sweeper. He was so small he couldn't even say the word 'sweep' properly.
- c 'That curled like a lamb's back
- d Tom's hair is compared to that of a lamb, suggesting he is young and gentle, just like a baby lamb.
- e Then down a green plain, leaping, laughing they run, And wash in a river and shine in the Sun.
- f This joyous image of the children playing reminds the reader of their youthful innocence, and suggests that they should be enjoying life rather than working in the dangerous job of chimney sweeping.

5
- a Hope of religious salvation is what encourages these young children to continue to work.
- b The vulnerability of children is emphasised, encouraging the readers to see them as precious and not as workers.
- c Death is a constant reality for these young children who are forced to work in such horrible conditions.

Structure pages 49–51

1
- a Poetry expresses an individual's most intense emotions in the least number of words.
- b 'I Wandered Lonely as a Cloud'
- c The beauty of nature, its freedom and the happiness nature brings to people

3
- a S: Wordsworth conveys the beauty of nature in his poem 'I Wandered Lonely as a Cloud'.
  T: He uses personification
  E: 'Beside the lake, beneath the trees, / Fluttering and dancing in the breeze'.
  E: This poetic device creates an image of the beautiful daffodils, dancing as if they were human.
  L: This technique encourages the reader to imagine the small flowers moving in the wind and therefore appreciate the joy that Wordsworth feels towards the beauty of nature.
- b beauty c creates, encourages d Furthermore

5
- a poetic devices, nature
- b William Wordsworth, 'I Wandered Lonely as a Cloud'
- c 1 beauty 2 freedom of nature 3 happiness to people

Language feature pages 52–53

1
- b image, elation c Determination, apathy
- d establishment, expectations
- e Cynicism f images, illness

2
- a anticipation b operation c judgment
- d amusement e hideousness f holiness
- g connotation h criticism

3
- b What time is our departure?
- c Mary's reaction made me laugh.
- d The length of Eliot's poem impressed me.
- e Ms MacRae could see the eagerness of her students.
- f The general feared that an enemy invasion was imminent.

Spotlight on spelling pages 53–54

1
- a illustrates b readers c stories
- d Shakespeare's e Plath's f Wordsworth's
- g children's h elves

2
- a authors' b painters' c illustrator's
- d filmmakers e poets f playwrights

3 (suggested answers)
- b The boys had hidden the girls' bags.
- c The engineer worked through the night to upgrade all of the computers' memories.
- d There's nothing more delightful than children's happiness.
- e I was inspired by the poem's natural imagery.

You be the teacher page 55

The innocence of children can lead to them being exploited by others. Blake's use of confronting imagery, 'my father sold me while yet my tongue could scarcely cry "'weep! 'weep! 'weep! 'weep!'" reminds the reader of the very young age at which the children were exploited. Furthermore, the sibilance of the line, 'So your chimneys I sweep & in soot I sleep' creates a sombre tone, making the reader feel complicit in the child's abuse. Blake effectively uses visual and aural images to communicate the idea that childhood innocence is abused by dishonest people.

UNIT 6 Radio interview transcripts

Understanding the question page 57

1 The act of writing the text for a play, film or radio interview.

2
- a A script includes references to speakers.
- b A script is for a spoken text.
- c A script is less descriptive.

3 youth homelessness: when a young person under the age of 24 has no fixed, regular or adequate housing

Planning and organisation pages 57–59

1 people who have been homeless, people who are homeless, psychologists, social workers, politicians, teachers

Structure pages 59–61

1 2, 1, 3

3 4, 3, 2, 1

Language feature pages 61–63

1 **a** light-hearted tone
Language features: first-person narrative, anecdote, colloquial language
Well, I can't speak for others, but my cat Charlie, he wakes me up at 4 am every morning [laughs]. He scratches at my door because he wants to be fed. I guess if that's as bad as it gets, cats are pretty good pets.

b factual tone
Language features: listing, statistics, objective language
There is a range of negatives associated with cat ownership. These negatives include unwanted pregnancy, health problems such as heartworm and feline cancer, not to mention the inevitable pain associated with the loss of a pet when they succumb to a paralysis tick. The average domestic cat costs over $1000 a year to keep, so for many families the biggest negative associated with cat ownership is cost.

c emotive tone
Language features: emotive language, hyperbole, adjectives
Cats could quite literally bring about the complete extinction of a number of small birds and mammal species. Irresponsible pet owners fail to desex their cats, resulting in unwanted litters which invariably are dumped in nature reserves and state parks. These feral cats are horribly disruptive to our already vulnerable native species.

2 **a** casual **b** anxious **c** sarcastic
d authoritative **e** sad **f** confident

3 (suggested answers)
b anxious: It's really stressful because no one knows whether they will get into university or get a job.
light-hearted: I can't wait until school is over because it will just be party, party, party.
c amused: They're great to have around—they jump up and say hello and generally just make us feel happy.
annoyed: There's nothing more frustrating than dogs being let off their leash by their inconsiderate owners.
d Topic: Working out at the gym
casual: I go to the gym when I've got time but I'm not too worried if weeks pass without me going.
serious: There has been a steep rise in the number of young men and women working out at the gym at least five times per week.

Spotlight on spelling pages 63–64

1 **a** saucepan **b** output **c** software
d checkout **e** sunshine **f** hardware
g greenhouse **h** upturn **i** onlooker

2 **a** takeoffs **b** attorneys-general
c brothers-in-law **d** sergeants major
e passers-by **f** hangers-on
g handfuls **h** mouthfuls

You be the teacher page 65

Interviewer: What are some causes of youth homelessness?
Interviewee: There are many reasons why young people become homeless. The primary factor is a lack of stability in the family home. There are a variety of reasons why home life may be unstable, including domestic violence, poverty and family breakdown. Other known reasons why young people find themselves homeless are mental illness, drug or alcohol abuse or lack of affordable housing.

UNIT 7 Magazine articles

Understanding the question page 67

1 to investigate something systematically

2 to record something in written, photographic or other form

3 **a** weight loss, muscle-building foods
b melting Arctic ice, diet of koalas
c breastfeeding tips, new toys for toddlers
d growing citrus fruits, how to make the best compost

Structure pages 69–71

1 **a** vii **b** ii **c** iii **d** iv **e** vi **f** i **g** v

2 **a** first-person narrative, personal experiences, anecdotes, rhetorical question, humour
b formal language, third-person narrative, sophisticated vocabulary, complex sentences

4 Best-selling young-adult fiction authors
First-time novelists intrigue young readers

5 **a** iii **b** v **c** iv **d** i **e** ii

7 (suggested answer)
Example three is the most effective as it summarises the main ideas of the article and finishes with a concluding comment.

Language features pages 71–73

1 **a** iii **b** vi **c** i **d** iv **e** ii **f** v

2 **a** iii **b** i **c** v **d** ii **e** iv

3 heartbreaking, tiny, ripped, crying, shocking

4 **b** disgusting (unhealthy)
c bullied (coerced)
d addicted (committed)
e pestered (questioned)
f agonised (deliberated)

Spotlight on spelling pages 73–74

1
- a caning
- b dosed
- c coming
- d abasement
- e miming
- f biting
- g paced
- h accurately
- i falsely
- j gently
- k gravely
- l lonesome

2
- a positively
- b correct
- c mining
- d correct
- e doting
- f hoped
- g correct
- h toting
- i timely
- j correct

You be the teacher page 75

Teenagers today have grown up indulging in daily access to a wide range of digital technologies. Many young people wake up in the morning and check their phones hopeful to find text messages, Facebook comments, likes on Instagram and retweets on Twitter. Once they are up and ready for the day, teenagers move on to school where they access technology, such as iPads and laptops, designed to positively enhance their learning. This sustained use of technology may have a long-term impact on young people's health, something that researchers must begin to assess.

UNIT 8 Web pages

Understanding the question page 77

1 divisive, contentious, provocative

2 (suggested answers)
Television: Shaun Micallef
Music: Madonna
Politics: Bill Clinton

Structure pages 79–81

1 2, 4, 1, 3

2 (suggested answer)
The controversial boxer Muhammad Ali was born Cassius Marcellus Clay Jnr. He converted to Islam in his 20s, when he adopted the name he is now famous for. Ali is a three-time World Heavyweight Champion and Olympic gold medallist. His outgoing personality earned him many fans, but also created controversy. He is well known for his flamboyant expressions, including, 'Float like a butterfly, sting like a bee.'

4 2, 4, 1, 3

6
- a northeast Tibet
- b 15
- c Lhamo Dhondup was only two years old when religious officials identified him as the reincarnation of the 13th Dalai Lama.
- d ii Finding the Dalai Lama

Language feature pages 81–82

1
- a factual
- b factual
- c opinion
- d opinion
- e factual
- f opinion

2
- a New Year's Day celebrations are enjoyed by many, especially the fireworks display on Sydney Harbour.
- b Many players fake injuries to get penalties in soccer matches.
- c It might surprise some that many people play video games professionally.
- d Mother Theresa inspires many people to be kind every day.

3
- a In my opinion, there is no other innovator as important to the 21st century as Steve Jobs.
- b My favourite sportsperson is the amazing and talented Muhammad Ali who fought against racial and religious prejudice.
- c The outrageous fashion of singer Lady Gaga makes her a powerful idol for many young artists, including myself.
- d I believe Michael Jackson's childhood was disturbed and led to his unhealthy obsession with people and objects in adulthood.
- e The brave and intelligent American president Barack Obama challenged the old-fashioned attitudes and ideas of many Americans.

Spotlight on spelling pages 83–84

1
- a adolescent
- b transferred
- c simultaneously
- d immediately
- e occasionally
- f desperate
- g approximately
- h embarrass

2
- a miscellaneous
- b privilege
- c lieutenant
- d desperate
- e defiantly
- f appreciate
- g tremendous
- h literally

3
- a separate
- b appreciate
- c all correct
- d conscious
- e all correct
- f definitely, tragedy
- g manoeuvres
- h amateur

You be the teacher page 85

Born Marshall Bruce Mathers III in October 1972, Eminem has emerged as one of the most controversial musicians of all time. His early life was unstable, especially his adolescence, as he was brought up in a low-income, single-parent family in Michigan. His interest in hip-hop started in his early teens and this was when he started using the name 'M&M', later to transform into the stage name 'Eminem'.

UNIT 9 Fan fiction stories

Understanding the question page 87

1
- **a** devotee or enthusiast
- **b** literature that describes imaginary people, places and events
- **c** an account of imaginary or real people and events told for entertainment

Structure pages 90–91

1 dialogue, detailed description of a place, action verbs, mix of sentence lengths

3 4, 2, 1, 3

Language feature pages 92–93

1
- **a** romance
- **b** royalty
- **c** evil or death
- **d** death or evil
- **e** money
- **f** new beginning

2
- **a** romance or love
- **b** happiness or hope
- **c** bad omen
- **d** hope or optimism
- **e** life

Spotlight on spelling pages 93–95

1
- **a** aren't
- **b** That's
- **c** isn't
- **d** don't
- **e** their
- **f** Whose
- **g** Balin's

2

didn't	they'll	they'd	he'd
weren't	hasn't	hadn't	who's
I've	we've	he'll	they'd
would've	it's	you're	they're

- **a** They'd
- **b** it's
- **c** we've
- **d** would've
- **e** didn't
- **f** hasn't
- **g** I've

You be the teacher page 96

Scully bent down to look closely at the small, oddly shaped footprints pressed lightly into the damp soil. As she bent, her ginger hair fell softly over her eyes. This slight movement wasn't dramatic, yet it made Mulder's heart beat a tiny bit faster than it should've. He turned away, bringing his eyes to the same prints Scully was now intently measuring. They mustn't be distracted from the task at hand. After all, no one else was willing to devote their lives to solving the mysteries hidden deep in the *X Files*.

UNIT 10 Protest poems

Understanding the question page 98

1 protest: a statement in disagreement with something
bullying: to use superior strength or force to intimidate someone

2 (suggested answer) climate change, education, violence against women, racism, sexism

Structure pages 100–101

1
- **a** Someone who knows someone with a disability
- **b** frustrated, emotional
- **c** (suggested answer) The most powerful line in the poem is when he is wrongly judged next time because the verb judged combined with the adverb wrongly reminds the reader that people with disabilities are frequently subjected to prejudice.

Language feature pages 101–103

1 **a** 8 **b** 16 **c** 4 **d** 14

2
b x / x / x / x /
You fool! You brute! You selfish farce!
iambic pentameter

c / x / x / x / x
Sing it softly, sing it loudly.
trochaic pentameter

d x / x / x / x /
The birds fall from the shattered sky.
iambic pentameter

3 trochaic tetrameter
Are we just birds screeching away?

iambic hexameter
The pain which they all feel I do not wish to feel

iambic dimeter
Don't step too fast.

trochaic pentameter
Join hands, rise up, the time to fight is now.

Spotlight on spelling pages 103–104

1
- **a** watching
- **b** swimming
- **c** hopping
- **d** admitting
- **e** scattering
- **f** panning
- **g** barring
- **h** arriving
- **i** dating
- **j** damaging
- **k** recycling

2
- **a** echoing
- **b** raining
- **c** encompassing
- **d** flattening
- **e** evading
- **f** travelling
- **g** shipping
- **h** hoping
- **i** listening
- **j** blotting
- **k** cleansing
- **l** chatting
- **m** fading

You be the teacher page 105

Images haunt me late at night,
Breaking my sleep with fear and fright.
Stopping my shallow breaths
Are pictures of their deaths.

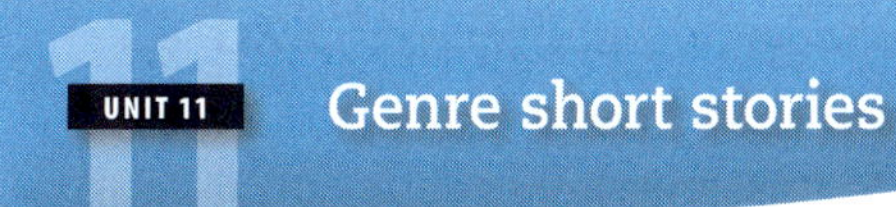

UNIT 11 Genre short stories

Understanding the question page 107

1 an intense feeling of fear or shock

2 fantasy, science fiction, comedy, romance, action, thriller

Planning and organisation pages 108–109

2 (possible answers) *Frankenstein*, *The Sixth Sense*, *The Raven*, *Nightmare on Elm Street*, *Scream*

4 (possible answers) graveyard, dungeon, remote castle, empty house, hospital

5 ghost—*antagonist* butcher—*antagonist*
vampire—*antagonist* teenager—*protagonist*
little girl—*protagonist* witch—*antagonist*
bride—*protagonist* scientist—*antagonist*
writer—*protagonist* zombie—*antagonist*

Structure pages 110–113

2 a iv b iii c ii d v e i

5 a man vs environment b man vs supernatural
c man vs self d man vs man

7 a iii b i c ii

Language features pages 113–116

1 a character b plot
c character and plot d character e plot

2 a ii b vi c vii d iii e i f v g iv h viii

3 unearthly: unnatural in a disturbing way
menacing: suggesting danger
suspense: the state of feeling uncertain, nervous and excited
dread: to anticipate something with fear
horrendous: extremely unpleasant
wraith: a ghostlike image of a person seen just before their death
wretched: a very unhappy or unfortunate person
phantom: a ghost or figment of someone's imagination
ghoul: a ghost or phantom that preys on dead bodies
ominous: the feeling that something bad will happen soon

5 a ghoul b wind c door
d gate e chair f leaves
g beast h child i cat
j ghost k high heels

6 a ii b vi c iv d ix e vii f viii g iii h i i v

7 (suggested answers)
a skull: Someone is going to die soon.
b cross: Faith in God will overcome evil.
c storm: Something bad will happen soon.

Spotlight on spelling pages 116–117

1 a skinny b smelly c sunny
d lumpy e bumpy f breezy
g messy h tasty i scary

2 a monstrous b spacious c mythical
d cautious e hysterical
f acrobatic g delicious

You be the teacher page 118

Clouds started covering the moon as I arrived at the terrible place where John was being held captive. An icy wind was blowing, and I rubbed my aching frozen fingers under my armpits. Standing in front of the imposing wooden door, I dared not try to imagine what lay beyond. Taking a deep breath of cold air, I pushed open the creaky door and disappeared into the gloomy darkness.

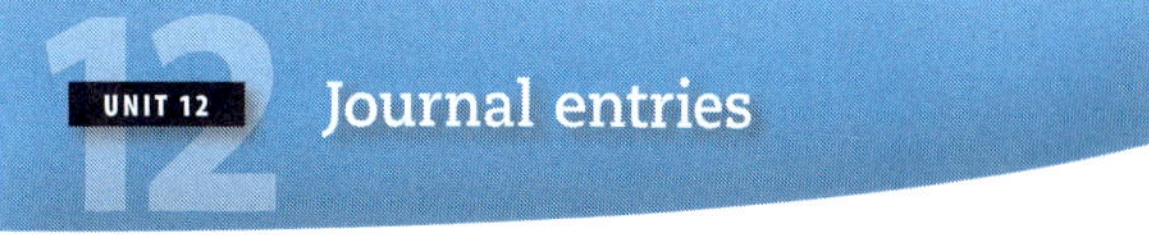

UNIT 12 Journal entries

Understanding the question pages 120–121

1 a a person who has expert knowledge of one or more scientific fields
b a daily record of news and events in a person's life
c to think deeply or carefully
d the act of being discovered

2 a ii, viii b i, x c vi, xii d iv, xi e iii, v f vii, ix

Structure pages 123–125

1 (suggested answers)
a The machine failed again, and it feels unlikely that it will ever work.
b I can't believe it worked!
c Jonathan insisted that he carefully checked the amount of water he put in the engine, but he couldn't have.
d I did not expect it but before my very eyes unfolded the most magical spectacle.
e I've never had a more satisfying day than today.

3 a sleeping chamber, flickering candle
b since before the sun peeped over the mountains, near 5 am, around mid-morning, autumn
c rather interesting, some might say amusing, my restless mind, frustration, found myself enjoying

4 5, 2, 3, 1, 4, 6, 7

Language features pages 125–127

1 b simple sentences, negative words and phrases, references to specific emotions
c sarcasm, exclamation
d criticism, exclamation

2 a I have no idea what this will mean for my career; will I be successful?
b The atoms' behaviour is just so unexpected—I can't understand why they have interacted in that way!
c The lunar eclipse occurs tonight and I can't wait!
d I've never seen a heart as large as this and I am eager to dissect it to discover the cause of its enlargement.
e optimistic: I believe that I am only a few days away from discovering the true cause of dreams.

3 a personification b metaphor
c simile d metaphor
e simile f personification
g simile h metaphor
i personification

4 (suggested answers)
b The light of the lamp was as bright as the sun.
c The computer's engine screamed.
d The blood-like ink of my pen dripped onto the page.
e The tea stung my lips like a wasp.

5 (suggested answers)
a A scientist is a cog in the machine of human knowledge.
b My assistant is a sloth.
c The sun rose like a fiery ball of steel.
d Every part of my body felt like it was weighed down by lead.

Spotlight on spelling page 128

1 a cheerful, cheerfully b careful, carefully
c deceitful, deceitfully d dreadful, dreadfully
e plentiful, plentifully f forceful, forcefully
g frightful, frightfully

2 a disgracefully b boastful
c fanciful d helpful
e mercifully f pitifully
g regretfully h beautifully

You be the teacher page 129

By 8 pm, the weather was perfect for searching the sky with my telescope. I had my telescope directed to where I knew Venus—my wonderful planet of love—resided. Looking deeply and carefully into the lens, I discerned that the planet had indeed moved. There she was! The new lens is much more powerful than my first one! At this point my heart began to race quite rapidly. Could this be the evidence that Venus has an atmosphere?